DEAD WEST WALKING:

Masculine Values and

Survival Principles for The

Decline

ALSO BY STEVEN FRANSSEN:

Rise And Fight: Defeat Globalism, Save The West

Make Self-Knowledge Great Again

Band of Visionaries

DEAD WEST WALKING

Masculine Values and Survival Principles for The Decline

STEVEN FRANSSEN

stevenfranssen.com

twitter.com/stevefranssen

youtube.com/c/stevenfranssen

All text, Copyright ©2019 by Steven Franssen

All Rights Reserved. No part of this book may be reproduced or transmitted in any form or by any means whatsoever without express written permission from the author, except in the case of brief quotations embodied in critical articles and reviews. Please refer all pertinent questions to the publisher.

To all the sane ones out there.

INTRODUCTION	1
PREPARING FOR THE DECLINE	16
MASS MIGRATION AND CULTURAL DECLINE	38
JUNK IN, JUNK OUT	45
DOMESTICATION	53
MASCULINITY AND PARENTING	61
THE ZOOMER WORLDVIEW	89
MAKING FRIENDS & BUILDING COMMUNITY	97
ENEMIES WITHIN	105
MALE BONDING	128
DIASPORA MINDSET	134

Introduction

"Including children, grandchildren and great-grandchildren, the average American woman will have 14 descendants.

The average African woman will have 258.

We all know what is coming.[1]" -Stefan Molyneux

The United Nations' Food and Agriculture Organization has predicted that the world's population will reach 9.1 billion by 2050 and the world needs to produce 70 per cent more food to feed all these extra people. This is not an impossible task but with IQ rates across the West plummeting, will the low IQ Third World step up to bat and deliver? It is highly unlikely.

Resources are finite and human needs are infinite.

Food shortages are coming. Food prices in the United States are steadily rising. Food price inflation has hovered somewhere around 2% for the past 10 years[2]. A loaf of organic, whole grain bread cost $3 in 2009. The same loaf now costs $4 in 2019. Our northern neighbor Canada is currently faced with a food price inflation crisis. With the country set to bring in 1 million new migrants from the

---

[1] https://www.coursehero.com/file/p3ejki/Longevity-and-Population-Growth-Death-rates-show-the-same-pattern-of-racial/
[2] https://tradingeconomics.com/united-states/food-inflation

Third World in the next three years[3], we can easily envision food riots in Canadian cities. Any disruptions in trucking and shipping to either Canada or America's more populated centers will be catastrophic. Automation of trucking via driverless trucks will lead to centralization of the industry, given our current corporate-capitalist system, and expose food delivery to electronic attack or disruptions from increasingly partisan corporations. Increasing prices and reducing deliveries to white, conservative regions will become as simple as a few mouse clicks. This possibility increases as coastal corporations become more and more populated by fiercely leftist Third Worlders enshrined with citizenship by the United States' standardless immigration system.

The specter of sectarian conflicts or even race war is ever present. Good borders make for good neighbors has been forgotten. Vicious fighting has resulted whenever this principle has been undermined. Orthodox white Christians in Ukraine were starved to death by a Russian and Jewish-led Soviet Union in the 1930's as part of an attempt to exterminate a people in order to replace them with another. The Rwandan genocide saw a Hutu government murder 70% of the Tutsi population, to the tune of 1 million souls. The Ottoman Empire, which held a large Muslim population, saw horrendous fighting over a century ago before being broken up into separate nations by foreign powers.

America will face its own sectarian violence. The precursors are already making the news. We see images of young white men in Make America Great Again hats being chased by mobs of non-whites. The run up to the 2016 election featured baying mobs of Third Worlders screaming in the faces of young white families. Catholic

---

[3] https://www.cicnews.com/2018/04/canadas-2018-2020-immigration-plan-is-a-step-in-right-direction-but-more-work-is-needed-0410485.html#gs.9XPOmayy

school boys recently underwent verbal assault by Black Israelites and crowding by Native Indians pounding drums. Middle aged whites are sucker punched in vicious attacks called "the knockout game" by blacks. Black on white crime is far outstripping the inverse. Blacks and Hispanics are fighting mob battles at public schools across the Los Angeles Unified School District, where Hispanics now hold a 70% majority. Hordes of low IQ Somali Muslims are inhabiting enclaves that are virtual no-go zones for outsiders, in Michigan and Minnesota. Rural, white Christian farmers in North Dakota, South Dakota, Montana, and Idaho are bringing in African blacks on work visas as reports of attacks on whites in these areas quietly increase. Africans show up in more and more places you wouldn't expect them. Entire small cities in Washington state and Oregon have become Hispanic. Chinese real estate investors are taking over large swaths of housing in Texas, Florida, Georgia, and California[4] and bringing with them ethnic nepotism and cultural practices from their homelands. The list of developments goes on and on.

A virulently anti-white and anti-conservative mainstream media reigns over the country. Peaceful attempts at undoing this evil power are tempered by the media war chest, totaling in the billions, and the partisan management of social media companies - all too happy to assist the media in libeling and de-personing of any and all political dissidents.

Not only is America all but assured sectarian violence, the mainstream narrative encourages it with race baiting in response to every major social event that makes the public eye.

---

[4] https://www.cnbc.com/2019/01/08/chinese-middle-class-buying-up-american-residential-real-estate.html

A great struggle is underway for the reigns of state power. The thuggish political demagoguery of the Third World makes headway in the House and soon the Senate. Mayoral and gubernatorial campaigns feature more and more Third Worlders, financed by Boomer Democrats who made out like bandits in the 1980's and 1990's before shackling their own children with billions of dollars in student loan debt. The 2020 Democratic field for President will feature minorities of every shape and color, each of them armed with taxation and social policies that will aim to finally undo once and forever the notion of America as a white nation. The intelligence agencies have been infected by political correctness and as of early 2019, are all helmed by women. Demographic voting patterns reveal a hardened commitment to socialism by black, Hispanic, Jewish, and Asian minorities.

Western Civilization being overrun by the fertile Africans, ascendant Muslims, and vigorous Hispanics will lead places like Tennessee, Illinois, and Connecticut to appear not as bucolic American states of yore but as multiethnic battle grounds reminiscent of modern-day South Africa. When government revenues falter and the central bankers run out of tricks, there will be no fresh avenues of funds for police forces to enforce multiculturalism. Policing will fall back to the most passive districts, allowing for ethnic enclaves to run wild. The most docile peoples will be the only ones capable of funding their own policing, as funding the policing of outgroups in a targeted manner is politically incorrect - despite the demographic crime statistics. Sharia courts will preside over Minnesota, Michigan, New Jersey, and Arkansas. Hispanic gangs will run the justice system in states like Iowa and Oklahoma. Asian bankers will dominate the West Coast, Jewish bankers the East. Whites will retreat more and more into the mountains and away from the urban centers. Taxation policies aimed specifically at whites will be enacted by Democratic legislatures in order to "right the wrongs of colonialism". The myth of climate change will fuel the myth of "climate refugees". White children will be taken from their white parents, especially from their fathers. The guise of "toxic masculinity" will be used as a weapon against straight, white male children in order to turn them into homosexuals. African gangs will stalk the lawless streets looking for plunder, rapine, and violence. No city over 50,000 in population will be safe for whites to inhabit.

This isn't "racism". These are just the facts. "Racism" is a word invented by Leon Trotsky in the 1920's to bludgeon white men over the head for noticing their imminent demise. There is a war on noticing, even among so-called "conservatives" within the ranks. Any single word of opposition to the conquest of whites by outgroups is shouted out by the low IQ grifters, warriors, and welfare queens of the Third World. Paul Joseph Watson is a near criminal in the UK for asking, "Is it conservative to give giant corporations huge tax breaks so they can import vast quantities of people from the third world and pay them slave wages while white Americans addicted to opioids live lives of atomized, nihilistic hopelessness?[5]" The fact that the term "reverse racism" exists is enough to cue any relatively intelligent white into the idea that "racism" is a term reserved exclusively for use against whites.

When the statistical averages reveal it's the majority of several races voting for the left and *one* race alone remains committed overall to smaller government, it's not so much a left-right conflict anymore[6]. There's a war on noticing this. Whites are not allowed to make any legal or even free market assurances for their own continued existence. Any who dare attempt to do this are hounded as fragile, racist, autistic, supremacist, pathetic, or hateful. Any psychologizing

---

[5] https://twitter.com/PrisonPlanet/status/1105131659786141696
[6] http://www.pewresearch.org/fact-tank/2018/11/08/the-2018-midterm-vote-divisions-by-race-gender-education/

will do so long as the white man is targeted, isolated, and removed from public discourse. The media concentrate all their years of training in persuasion to depict the white man who is racially aware as a frothing buffoon. The media is all too happy to dredge up whatever low IQ white man who *actually* hates other races in order to place him alongside the sophisticated man who simply wants to build onto what he inherited. Guilt by association. Any psychological game works so long as it stupefies the masses and buys more time for those who are importing the Third World into the West.

This book is a discussion of the developing circumstances of America's decline, the importance of proper masculinity and parenting despite these circumstances, the types of people who could disrupt masculinity and parenting, and what some of the West's most resilient groups have done when faced with similar odds.

Pre-1965 Immigration Act, America used to have a national identity. The people were predominantly English Protestants, the common language was English and only English, people went to church on Sunday, country music throbbed in the heart of America, despite the Democrats holding the House the GOP was the party assumed to be a powerhouse in the generations to come, apple pies cooled on window sills, a man could make a decent living, support a family, and buy a home with just a few years wages, men cooled off in the evenings over a beer at fraternal clubhouses, and *Made In The USA* was everywhere you shopped. America had folk heroes like Davey Crockett, Andrew Jackson, and the Founding Fathers. The former Confederate states were treated with dignity. Families were intact, blacks were raising themselves out of poverty by 1% a year, and America was a shining beacon of freedom for Europeans who aspired to spread the values of liberty to their own shores. Western values flowed outward and Americans were esteemed wherever they went.

America has little identity now. It has become a shopping mall of squabbling ethnicities, administrated by Goldman Sachs and one President Kushner. Everyone knows this but few dare speak it. English Protestants are a small sliver of the population and are expected to feed the Third World and adopt as many African children as possible. Degenerate hip hop with performers moonlighting at pornography conferences have become the institutional norm. The Democrats are in a waiting game with the GOP, knowing the demographics will be on their side in no time. Apple pies no longer adorn window sills because the Kushner/Trump economy has placed special emphasis on getting Millennial women into the workforce. The Boy Scouts have become the Gender-Neutral Scouts Where Girls Are Preferred. Everything is made in China (thanks, Clinton!). America's heroes are now whatever spineless idiot Marvel or D.C. Comics puts forward. Most of the Confederate statues have been torn down by liberal college students or disgruntled mayors. Families are falling apart because of the opioid epidemic. Blacks are hypnotized by ghetto culture and purveyors like Jay-Z, Hillary Clinton, Jesse Jackson, and Kamala Harris. America can no longer rely on a steady stream of conservatives from Europe since Europe is on the brink of mass collapse and full civil war. Rather than flow outwardly, Western values are denigrated at every turn by a greedy media.

America is now America, Inc. The government has ballooned so far out of size that it does not resemble in the slightest the will of the American people. American national identity is so far displaced that Obama nearly succeeded in killing off 4th of July fireworks celebrations across the country and nary a whimper was raised in any significant public platform[7]. With a controlled media, it was by design.

With Trumpism, national identity is making a comeback. Trumpism may have even become corrupted by Grifters, Inc. but the grassroots enthusiasm still remains. Whether the idiots running the GOP are displaced by their more vigorous, immigration-woke counterparts is yet to be seen. Matt Schlapp, who runs CPAC, and his wife Mercedes Schlapp, who is the White House Director of Strategic Communications, have had a big hand in influencing Donald Trump away from his campaign message of less immigration to a Jeb Bush-like parroting of Big Business talking points. Trump is betraying his base and he may just end up with nothing to show at the end of his Presidency for defying the entire establishment in order to serve Real America. Less Kushner, more Stephen Miller is the ticket. And doesn't it all always boil down to immigration and state power?

Populism is powered by the universal principle of "nation first" and some would say "humanity first". Outside loyalties are quickly falling out of fashion, despite the media's best efforts to gaslight the general populace. Stefan Molyneux writes, "Whites enslaved others the least. Whites enslaved others for the shortest amount of time. Whites ended slavery around the world. Only whites are blamed for slavery. Trying to save the world is destroying whites. You know it. I know it. So STOP IT![8]" Whites have been lied to by the globalist tribe into believing their loyalties must first and foremost be given to an outside tribe, blacks. As such, the whites have spent untold billions and thousands of years of human labor in the service of blacks. This has eroded the self-sufficiency of blacks and put whites on a course far from the natural order. Were it not for the insane

---

[7] https://www.teaparty.org/fireworks-industry-fights-back-host-obama-regs-105601/

[8] https://twitter.com/StefanMolyneux/status/1097380819520221184

propaganda job of the globalists on the Western world, whites would be exploring space right now and blacks would have pulled themselves out of poverty and claimed their own unique destiny. Globalism has been a great big lie which has resulted in mob rule, where the individual loses to the tribe every time. There must be a peaceful separation of the tribes, a massive reduction in state power, and return to "nation first" as the operating principle of socio-political organization so that healthy individualism can elevate tribes to their highest possible ideals. This is the true diversity hidden so far from sight.

History is an endless parade of different groups killing one another over disputes that could not be resolved through peaceful means. Moral culpability for these endless conflicts has generally been spread across the parties involved, though there are a few examples of genuinely evil forces aligning against good. This battle of globalism vs. nationalism is an example. Communism has killed over 100 million people and there could be absolute rivers of blood all over the West if the globalists have their way. They are busy setting the races against each other by activating racial animosities through ideological propaganda, racial hate crime hoaxes, inflamed rhetoric, selective reporting, and government sanctioned mass migration. This is the final showdown between good and evil and these are End Times. The globalists know the composition of history. They know that different groups in too close of proximity inevitably war with one another. They wish to provoke sectarian violence while hiding back in the shadows, accumulating capital and security forces with which to run over the remaining combatants when the dust has settled. They would seize the economy and turn the survivors into out and out livestock living in permanent serfdom. According to some, these globalists want to build a breakaway society. They do not want to share. They want to fulfill their Satanic vision of global chaos so as to impose their own order. They will live in super compounds guarded by the most elite technology. They will carouse in their compounds, consuming the blood of the youngest tax livestock[9], extending their own lifespans, and eventually trying to make interstellar or interdimensional contact in order to try and serve a darker power than themselves.

We are not dealing with "Gauls vs. Romans" or "Spaniards vs. Incans" here. We are dealing with harbingers of permanent darkness. Overwhelming technological advances have poised the globalists for permanent takeover. There is no happy ending if they win in the next generation. The average person will be under constant monitoring, threat of kidnapping by artificially intelligent drones, and all manner of deracination, castration, and castigation for the slightest of deviations from acceptable thought. The post-apocalyptic world of the Terminator film series will look like a cakewalk compared to the havoc the globalists intend to unleash. At least the rebels in the Terminator universe had the intelligence to fight back. The globalists have already positioned themselves to have complete control over the planetary fresh water supply[10] and will happily "turn the frogs gay" at will.

The answer to longstanding white guilt and subservience to blacks is not for white man to punish the blacks with a race war, or vice versa. The answer is disentanglement and a bulldog's throat grip onto the jugular of the globalist cabal. Time is against the West as the globalists are deliberately plunging IQ levels down into the low 80's, the sweet spot for criminality. The most intelligent have an absolute moral imperative to procreate vigorously and populate the planet with

---

[9] "Peter Thiel Wants To Inject Himself With Young People's Blood"
https://www.vanityfair.com/news/2016/08/peter-thiel-wants-to-inject-himself-with-young-peoples-blood

[10] https://popularresistance.org/wall-street-mega-banks-are-buying-up-the-worlds-water/

more people who will resist the coming darkness. Even if whites are dislodged from the West to the point of being a diaspora, hope must live on so that the ultimate global pandemic of globalist victory can be pushed back and eventually eradicated from consciousness.

The bizarro world of flipped moral values posited by the media arm of the globalist cabal has attempted to convince the healthiest of Westerners to stop procreating while contributing their hard-earned monies directly into the mouths of those most genetically and mentally prone to violence. Global takeover is the endgame of generations of accumulated capital obtained by ill-gotten means. The super wealthy influence the course of human action. The slightest problem in their personality puts whole fields of psychological and financial distortions onto the world. They achieve their global chaos and breakaway society only if we, the moral people of the world, fail in our mission to combat their evil. There is still hope but all men must wake up to the division sewn between the races. Let the West balkanize but don't let the West devolve into open race war. Peaceful separation keeps nationalism alive and gives the better angels of our nature a shot at finally driving Satan back to Hell where he belongs.

It is no surprise that toxic femininity has dislodged masculinity from its rightful place in the world. All the wars between men stretching back tens of thousands of years have killed around one billion humans. The nagging feminists having succeeded in the legal enshrinement of abortion. 1.5 billion humans have died from abortion in the past 40 years. The inversion of moral values brought on by globalism has unleashed an insidious violence of such proportions that men could not have possibly achieved at the helm of civilization. The mobilization of men against men deals in might versus might. Women have been mobilized against children and the men have been stunned into paralysis by political correctness. The runaway slaughter of children continues unabated, the Republic of Ireland[11] being one of the latest to join the ranks of the infanticidal. Irish men were stunned into paralysis by a globalist, Indian homosexual named Leo Varadkar -who led the drive for legalization of abortion. How fitting! The pattern of toxically feminine political figures slipping past the defenses of moral men in order to induce the local women into infanticide can be seen across the West. In his deep nihilism resulting from a choice to ally with Communism in order to genocide the Germans after the Second World War, Western man lacks the political will to bring this new breed of evildoer to justice. We cannot accept this state of affairs. This is the importance of the resurgence of masculinity.

There can be no moral will toward virtue if every man's testicles have been zapped by toxins in the environment and his brains have been washed by moral lectures from toxically feminine political figures financed to the gills by central bankers. True masculinity means ungodly hard work, sobriety, virtuous parenting, physical and hormonal health, impulse control, hierarchy, and war against evil. Good men must convince good men to have plenty of good children and all must struggle against the civilization wreckers. Female evil must be reined in at all costs. A man does well to surround himself with men who are capable warriors. Cobbling together a wormy group of Gammas is a stupid plan for making it through the American decline. Choosing an Alpha leader, robust Betas, and committed, tough Deltas is the way to go. For an Alpha, this is a recruitment process where a man's masculinity and ability to grasp the existential seriousness of the situation is scrutinized. Will the man fight when the time comes? Will he practice courage under

---

[11] https://www.theguardian.com/world/2018/may/27/ireland-to-start-abortion-law-reform-after-historic-vote

fire, or will he spend his life foolishly and put others at risk? Will he hang back and complain, or will he take charge and follow the reasoning? These considerations will matter more and more as war goes from the far-off Middle East to the city streets of major US liberal cities and their outlying suburbs. A new generation of warfare is coming where the combatants will not be uniformed soldiers but Average Joes fighting against all comers. This is already taking place in France, Sweden, the UK, and Germany. Plenty of violence is to come and the American elite have ensured it by bringing in Mexicans instead of Scandinavians for 50 years. The quality of the men in a brotherhood, gang, or tribe determines their survivability. More on this in the masculinity section of the book.

Networking with people who share your values is the surest way to get along when the going gets rough. A capitalist who surrounds himself with socialists will be the first to lose all his money when the socialists take power. Unless he is succeeded by a Republican or reasonable independent, President, Donald J. Trump will spend his twilight years prosecuted by every kangaroo court the Democrats can conceive of. This was his sacrifice. Some people have to live this way, especially when political power is a concern. Those of us who are not directly positioned to take political power have more wiggle room. Our lives are not quite so forfeit. We have the choice to relate to virtuous people and build working relationships with them while the economy is still hot. Good people get us through the hard times. More on this in the section on building community.

Good parents need to network with other good parents in order to raise their kids with other reasonable kids. Parents who didn't network before their kid was of school age may be tempted to send their kids to public school or join a religious denomination outside of their beliefs in order to get their kid around other kids.

Better to save the heartache and have good people around by reaching out now to anyone who appears to have peaceful parenting values. More on this in the parenting section of the book.

White man has had as much a hand in his own imminent destruction as the outgroups. After all, it was the Boomer generation who fed the Third World with organizations such as Save The Children and Live Aid. It was the Boomer white man who universalized his empathy and compassion despite the never-ending lack of reciprocity on the part of the Third World. White man sowed the seeds of African birth rates upwards of 6 children per mother[12]. Even neoliberal rags such as The Economist have to concede that soaring African birth rates have contributed to jaw dropping poverty on the continent[13]. Yet, isn't it important to grant moral agency to those reproducing and consuming at unsustainable rates? White man has contributed considerably to his own predicament, to his prospect of annihilation.

Whites will need to have their "never again" moment, as the Ashkenazi Jews did with the Holocaust. Is white man due a genocide? Certainly not. In fact, tremendous amounts of gratitude are owed to the race of man that established civilization. For those who have been net contributors in their lifetimes, it is time to expect some gratitude from the Third World. Not only is the demographic assault against the West something to be diffused, there ought to be some gratitude in return. The only race to end slavery was whites and it came at the cost of 800,000 to 1,000,000 of America's finest men[14]. The only race in history to spend any amount of money to improve the lot of other

---

[12] https://www.statista.com/statistics/262884/countries-with-the-highest-fertility-rates/
[13] https://www.economist.com/middle-east-and-africa/2018/09/22/africas-high-birth-rate-is-keeping-the-continent-poor
[14] https://en.wikipedia.org/wiki/American_Civil_War

races has been the white race. Third Worlders pour into the West in order to be given free money. Does the generosity of the white race know no bounds?

The "never again" moment may be the loss of a great cultural or political figure through murder or assassination by an outgroup. It may be the wholesale genocide of the South African farmers currently surrounded on all sides by hostile, black Communists. It may be the detonation of a dirty bomb by a terrorist group in a major American metropolitan area. Or the "never again" moment may come through a revival of the 1960's race riots that gripped the nation just as cultural Marxism was taking flight. Perhaps it will come through the Presidential election of a non-white, anti-white who won't be as capable of hiding his or her racial vitriol as Barack Hussein Obama was able to. At some point, white people will have had enough.

The exclusive benefits of the elite's breakaway society must be universalized for the common person so that global IQ's can rise, hunger, disease, and poverty can truly be eradicated, and so that humanity can step into a new Golden Age of astonishing achievement, peace, and prosperity.

There is a lot of violence coming to the West, but it is my sincere hope with this book to prevent as much violence as possible without advocating for capitulation. The problems facing America need not be resolved through violence, but the hour is late. Let us use words while there is still time.

Preparing for The Decline

Poison Pills

The West is soon to be overrun by lower IQ people who reproduce at prodigious rates, have the highest rates of criminality, and vote at an extremely high clip for socialism. The spread of multiracialism touches all corners of the West: from tremendous amounts of Samoans in Anchorage, Alaska to Somali migrants flooding into Portland, Maine and overwhelming local resources, skyrocketing FBI rape statistics for the area in the process[15]. Well-meaning whites have crippled the West by erecting welfare states, running untold number of "feed the Third World" initiatives, and by electing Democrat leaders like Obama - who was all too happy to assist in the killing of bulwark strong men like Muammar Gaddafi. The strong men who once held back migrant invasions no longer live. They burn in Hell with the ghost of John McCain.

The rising tide of Third Worldism looks to continue unabated with President Donald J. Trump signing a spending bill in February 2019 that puts the final nail into America's coffin. Renowned American defense attorney and immigration commentator Daniel Horowitz writes:

> This bill contains a blatant amnesty for the worst cartel smugglers: Section 224(a) prohibits the deportation of anyone who is sponsoring an "unaccompanied" minor illegal alien – or who says they might sponsor a UAC, or lives in a household with a UAC, or a household that potentially might sponsor a UAC. It's truly difficult to understate the betrayal

---

[15] https://gellerreport.com/2019/01/maine-asylum-seekers.html/

behind this provision. One of the driving factors of the invasion is the misinterpretation of the UAC law. Under current law, Central American teenagers are only treated as refugees if they are A) a victim of "A severe form of trafficking" and B) have no relatives in the country. Yet almost all of them are self-trafficked by these very illegal relatives who are indeed present in the country. Rather than clamping down on this fleecing of the American people, the bill gives amnesty to the very people paying the cartels to invade us![16]

Unless something dramatic changes, this will have been a Jared and Ivanka Kushner presidency whose tagline was, "Goldman Sachs First". American decline is all but assured and it doesn't take a genius to predict civil war these days.

The lack of positive movement on the part of the Trump Administration was unexpected by many in the MAGA movement. His election campaign was singular in world history and elevated some of the best Americans to the fore: Ann Coulter, Tucker Carlson, Steve Bannon, Stephen Miller, Laura Loomer, etc. Trump immediately destroyed all his forward momentum going into his inauguration by hiring Never Trump staffers who proceeded to leak his every move to the press. He kept Sean Spicer as his Press Secretary for far too long, which is to say at all, and quickly ousted Steve Bannon when Bannon was too assertive about staying true to the original MAGA agenda. The only America First person who remains on staff for him is Stephen Miller, whose contributions we cannot be sure of. Senate Majority Leader Mitch McConnell has done his part to keep the donor base satisfied by dodging Trump on immigration only

---

[16] https://www.conservativereview.com/news/5-insane-provisions-amnesty-omnibus-bill/

to ram through tax cuts for corporations and other wealthy donors of the GOP. At this point, the best things the Trump administration has going for it is the prospect of putting another conservative on the Supreme Court bench, the overhaul of the judiciary with savvy appointments, and eventually putting up some distance of ineffective bollard-fencing along the southern border thanks to a National Emergency declaration that will take upwards of two years to wind its way through the courts. One News Now reports:

> Democrats have filed lawsuits challenging the president's declaration of an emergency. With California taking the lead, 16 states have filed a lawsuit challenging the president's emergency declaration to fund a border wall. Joining California Attorney General Xavier Becerra are the attorneys general of Colorado, Connecticut, Delaware, Hawaii, Illinois, Maine, Maryland, Michigan, Minnesota, Nevada, New Jersey, New Mexico, New York, Oregon, and Virginia. All the states involved in the lawsuit have Democratic attorneys general.[17]

Every one of those states has major demographic problems. A bright spot for America First is the fact that the most recent GOP members of Congress voted against the disastrous spending bill loaded to the gills with poison pills, including the aforementioned de facto amnesty. The final route left back to America First involves genuine firebrands making it to Congress in 2020, Trump barely squeaking through to a second Presidency because of a split vote between an independent and the Democrat, and some drastic change of White House personnel. Otherwise, the American people (those who remain) will be subjected to the election of a Democrat and immediate reversal of all Trump era reforms.

---

[17] https://onenewsnow.com/national-security/2019/02/19/democratic-ags-team-up-against-common-sense-barrier#.XGyaRKLvqYw.twitter

The Trump economy is currently piping hot. Recent Gallup polls indicate, "Some 69 percent told Gallup that they expect their personal finances to be even better next year, just shy of the record 71 percent when the internet boom was raging under former President Bill Clinton.[18]" Furthermore:

> The labor market has remained strong even as the recovery has stretched on toward a decade. In the past three months, the economy has added an average of 241,000 net new jobs a month, more than twice as much as needed to keep up with population growth and keep unemployment trending down. As a result, more of the population is working. For prime-age workers, meaning those between ages 25 and 54, the total employment rate rose to 79.9 percent in January, the highest such rate since the financial crisis hit.[19]

The economists like to lie and gin up Obama's meager job figures at the end of his term as some indication of his catalyzing the Trump economy. The truth is that Trump's moves to cut regulations, bring back jobs to America, cut taxes (however much for the rich), and to reinstill confidence in the American economy are all considerations ping-pong-playing Obama failed to make. When asked about the economy in 2016, Barack Hussein Obama sniveled and whined:

> When somebody says like the person you just mentioned (Trump) who I'm not going to advertise for, that he's going to bring all these jobs back. Well how exactly are you going to do that? What are you going to do? There's uh-uh no answer

---

[18] https://www.washingtonexaminer.com/washington-secrets/boom-best-economic-optimism-in-16-years-50-better-off-under-trump

[19] https://www.washingtonexaminer.com/policy/economy/job-openings-hit-record-high-of-7-3-million-in-december

to it. He just says. 'I'm going to negotiate a better deal.' Well how? How exactly are you going to negotiate that? What magic wand do you have? And usually the answer is, he doesn't have an answer.

Trump has had an answer and the statistics just don't lie. Even the globalist run NY Times has given Trump on the economy an "A-"[20].

The Trump economy is not likely to last. There are simply too many people pouring into the country at too fast a rate for wages to rise. The cost of labor goes down as more and more Third Worlders clamor for the jobs that American teenagers used to do at higher wages. This is great for bigtime employers, especially the ones propping up the feeble real estate sector. Another poison pill in the recent spending bill signed by Trump is explained to us by Daniel Horowitz:

> This bill (p. 1,161) doubles the number of H-2B non-agricultural, unskilled seasonal workers who will continue to be a public charge on America. This gives you a glimpse of what is driving this amnesty bill on the Republican side.[21]

Rather than force farm owners and construction companies to raise their wages by cutting off the supply of cheap foreign labor, the Republican-controlled Congress works for their wealthy donors by doubling the number of unskilled workers coming into the country! The GOP is rotten to the core, but no change need come when Trump happily signs anything Mitch McConnell puts in front of him. Farmers don't have to innovate, automate, or upskill because they can rely on the modern form of slave labor: cheap foreign workers.

---

[20] https://www.nytimes.com/2019/02/04/business/us-economy-trump-taxes-trade.html
[21] https://www.conservativereview.com/news/5-insane-provisions-amnesty-omnibus-bill/

Meanwhile, crime in their locales increases because Mexicans have a penchant for drug smuggling, marijuana grow operations, gang violence, and rape. Our new country is going to be great!

Life Vests and Lifeboats In Order

We all know what is coming: plenty of sectarian violence, banana republic style politics, food shortages, and massive government interventions in the economy. Bernie Sanders announced his candidacy for the Presidency earlier this month. He has his political machine from 2016 and more in store for Donald Trump. His polling blows runner up Kamala Harris out of the water and Bernie remains second in the polls only to Joe Biden, who has a penchant for whispering sexually into the ears of little girls. The Third Worlders and their white liberal handlers are loud and proud. Personal safety will become an area of uncertainty in a white minority America. Preparing now to minimize damage down the line is the operating motive for conservatives, and whites in general.

There are a thousand and one prepper books on Amazon worth perusing. I recommend the sometimes-strange *Survival Theory* by Jonathan Hollerman[22]. The book is chalk full of realistic scenarios, aside from the obvious racially motivated violent gangs of non-whites coming to your house in the middle of the night. The author is especially concerned with the vulnerability of the American power grid to electronic attack and writes extensively on countermeasures for food shortages and inclement weather. The world is already seeing

---

[22] Hollerman, J. (2016). Survival theory: A preparedness guide: How to survive the end of the world on a budget. McConnellsburg, PA: APOC Publishing.

extensive cyberattacks in failed socialist states like Venezuela leading to downed power grids[23]. There will be little to stop such occurrences in a United States that has failed due to socialism and central banking. I will leave prepper information up to the experts and direct you to a "prepper" search on YouTube for any tactical suggestions for surviving the decline. This book will help in that regard so far as mindset, sociopolitical awareness, and building community goes but we're going lite on the prepper fare for the duration.

Any person looking to safeguard their wellbeing into the future needs to participate right now in the Trump economy any way possible. Conservatives are starting to lose their jobs and get blocked out of financial services because of their political beliefs. White flight to safer havens is running out as conservatives cannot legally discriminate against hiring the liberals who bring multiculturalism with them. Now is the time to make money. Money buys weapons, food stores, property, water, ammunition, armor, drones, and other assets that will increase a person's survivability. As the day to day assurance of personal safety within America's borders drops, it is important not to flaunt one's wealth as it will turn one into a target for the redistributist mobs to come. Of course, the wealthiest will be able to afford private, armed security. This will not be the case for a lot of the upper middle class or even the middle class, especially as random violence escalates, and more and more moneyed people are picked off by the mob.

Let's say the Trump economy lasts...great! The borders don't look to close, mass *legal* migration will continue unabated, and the welfare state will not have been dismantled. Everyone will have plenty of money to fight over. People will still split off into their ethnic groups. The social pressures will get to America, one way or another.

---

[23] https://www.rt.com/news/453434-venezuela-maduro-cyberattack-power-grid/

Better to have spent all this while preparing and networking to be able to come into a slightly different set of social circumstances than an outright failed economy. The flavor of catastrophe is up to the whims of those at the helm of the Titanic as it smashes into the iceberg. Better to have your life vests and lifeboats in order.

The elite know this all too well and they are hedging their bets. Stuff, a New Zealand based publication, provides a look into the mindset of the elite:

> Wealthy Americans are buying property in New Zealand see the country as a "bolthole" in the event of a catastrophe, a Queenstown real estate executive says. Bayleys Queenstown executive director Stacy Coburn says Silicon Valley bosses and US hedge fund managers are buying property in the South Island as a safe place to hide in the event of a major terror attack. 'Queenstown is seen as a bolthole for the future if things do turn to the worse in the world,' he said.[24]

New Zealand's southern island, which just had a mass shooting in Christchurch[25], is geographically isolated from the rest of the West, has plenty of fresh water, is difficult for the masses to get to, and is more and more populated by elite prepper types. Peter Thiel, the most notable Donald Trump supporter in Silicon Valley, has had dual American-Kiwi citizenship since 2011. Thiel owns, "a 477-acre (193-hectare) lakefront estate in Wanaka on the South Island, is valued at $5.6 million," according to Fortune[26]. The New Yorker featured an extensive article on the elite prepper mindset:

---

[24] https://www.stuff.co.nz/business/88705064/super-rich-americans-buying-land-in-new-zealand-as-bolthole-from-apocalypse
[25] https://globalnews.ca/news/5058487/christchurch-shots-fired-mosque/
[26] http://fortune.com/2017/01/25/peter-thiel-new-zealand-citizenship/

How many wealthy Americans are really making preparations for a catastrophe? It's hard to know exactly; a lot of people don't like to talk about it. ("Anonymity is priceless," one hedge-fund manager told me, declining an interview.) Sometimes the topic emerges in unexpected ways. Reid Hoffman, the co-founder of LinkedIn and a prominent investor, recalls telling a friend that he was thinking of visiting New Zealand. "Oh, are you going to get apocalypse insurance?" the friend asked. "I'm, like, Huh?" Hoffman told me. New Zealand, he discovered, is a favored refuge in the event of a cataclysm. Hoffman said, "Saying you're 'buying a house in New Zealand' is kind of a wink, wink, say no more. Once you've done the Masonic handshake, they'll be, like, 'Oh, you know, I have a broker who sells old ICBM silos, and they're nuclear-hardened, and they kind of look like they would be interesting to live in.' I asked Hoffman to estimate what share of fellow Silicon Valley billionaires have acquired some level of "apocalypse insurance," in the form of a hideaway in the U.S. or abroad. "I would guess fifty-plus per cent," he said, "but that's parallel with the decision to buy a vacation home. Human motivation is complex, and I think people can say, 'I now have a safety blanket for this thing that scares me.'

The fears vary, but many worry that, as artificial intelligence takes away a growing share of jobs, there will be a backlash against Silicon Valley, America's second-highest concentration of wealth. (Southwestern Connecticut is first.) "I've heard this theme from a bunch of people," Hoffman said. "Is the country going to turn against the wealthy? Is it going to turn against technological innovation? Is it going to turn into civil disorder?[27]

With radical socialist politicians like Bernie Sanders, Ilhan Omar, Alexandra Ocasio Cortez, and Kamala Harris on the rise in the United States, these are valid questions to ask. A common sight on Twitter these days is immigrants to America calling for the radical redistribution of wealth and silencing of whites as their dispossession is carried out. The Silicon Valley elite are right to question the changing political atmosphere, though too many of them place far too much blame on the shoulders of Donald Trump. Also profiled in the New Yorker article is Larry Hall and his Survival Condo Project consisting of underground bunkers built in former nuclear silos and fallout shelters on the United States mainland. The author writes:

> "...we stopped at Hall's latest project—a second underground complex, in a silo twenty-five miles away. As we pulled up, a crane loomed overhead, hoisting debris from deep below the surface. The complex will contain three times the living space of the original, in part because the garage will be moved to a separate structure. Among other additions, it will have a bowling alley and L.E.D. windows as large as French doors, to create a feeling of openness. Hall said that he was working on private bunkers for clients in Idaho and Texas, and that two technology companies had asked him to design "a secure facility for their data center and a safe haven for their key personnel, if something were to happen." To accommodate demand, he has paid for the possibility to buy four more silos." The demand for condo space in these underground

---

[27] https://www.newyorker.com/magazine/2017/01/30/doomsday-prep-for-the-super-rich

redoubts is massive and most developments sell out before they have broken ground."

The average person is unable to pull off a complex fortification. Strategic relocation may be an option for some. The ten least population-dense states in the Union and their relative advantages and disadvantages are:

1. Alaska

Much ballyhooed on survivalist forums, Alaska offers healthy separation from the contiguous 48, plenty of natural resources, and a favorable tax situation for the middle class. The state also has complete homeschool freedom. With extensive military installations and robust welfare state, Alaska has attracted plenty of Third Worlders and lower 48 people who can't fit in with the rest of society - generally in ways that are unfavorable to the reasonable person looking for a redoubt. The elite of Alaska get by the best with remote lakeside mansions, helicopters, and small planes. Anchorage is a Mexican-Samoan cultural center where it's positively stupid to be outside after midnight. A prepper headed to Alaska will also have to contend with mosquitoes, odd sunshine and nightfall hours during summer and winter, crowding around the Anchorage area, a disgruntled moose here and there, and an Alaskan Native population with sky high alcoholism rates that has a defacto ethnostate in upper Alaska because of Federal legislative favors granted to them.

2. Wyoming

Wyoming is not favored on survivalist forums due to its short growing season, lack of arable land, unforgiving wind, understated invasion by Mexicans (particularly in southwest Wyoming), and the lack of diversity in the economy. When oil does well, Wyoming does well. Wyoming has a low tax burden, a lower cost of living compared to the coastal states, decent to outright good finance laws, and a low population density. Wyoming suffers from one of the same problems as the next two states on the list with Christian farmer types bringing in Africans on work visas and chain migration schemes to work at farms on rock bottom wages. Wyoming is projected to be one of the only solidly Republican states when whites become a minority in their own country around 2045. Liberals have recently targeted Wyoming for demographic change as it sends two Senators to the US Congress just as California does, despite their massive population disparity. A mega corporation like Amazon establishing headquarters in the state would be absolutely ruinous to the state's potential as a doomsday shelter for everyone but the elite.

Wyoming has lower homeschool regulations and recently passed a "Food Freedom Act" which permits the private sale of most foodstuffs besides meat without food inspection.

3. Montana

Montana is lower tax burden, has some natural resources, features the highest percentage of non-Hispanic whites of any state on this list and the lowest black population of any state in the US[28], and has less of a welfare state than many of the northeastern US states that have similar winters. Montana is also becoming a liberal haven not only because of the longstanding university presence in Missoula but more recently because of successful Republican efforts to bring the tech industry to Bozeman. The GOP lost an easily winnable Senate

---

[28] https://en.wikipedia.org/wiki/List_of_U.S._states_and_territories_by_African-American_population

race in 2018 because of the lack of winner candidates in the state and because Bozeman's Gallatin County has seen explosive, Democratic population growth. Montana is a solidly purple state filled with disaffected libertarians who routinely swing elections to Democrats. Montana may be pretty, but she is all too happy to whore herself out to out-of-state land developers and socialist Californians who expand her welfare state. High real estate costs, bad homeschool regulations requiring parents teach about the accomplishments of natives, and an overinvolved Highway Patrol are black marks against the state. Montana is Oregon minus the Mexicans...for now.

4. North Dakota

North Dakota is remote, flat, ugly to most, features severe alcoholism rates, dangerous winter road conditions, a lack of essential services, and those wonderful Christian farmers tasking themselves with saving Somalia through farm visas. Upsides include a low crime rate (which is changing on account of immigration), "boredom" because a lack of urban centers, plenty of grass-fed beef to fill up on, a somewhat decent tax burden, lucrative oil jobs when oil is up, and rock bottom real estate prices. North Dakota is constantly overlooked by the rest of the country, a factor well in its favor as a redoubt. Income will be a difficult prospect for anyone whose career isn't location independent.

North Dakota is a "food freedom" state but has prohibitive regulations on homeschooling.

5. South Dakota

Favorable conditions in South Dakota include one of the lowest costs of living in the nation (especially outside of western South Dakota), low business regulations, the seventh lowest tax burden[29], somewhat affordable real estate, more career options than North Dakota or Wyoming, relative geographic isolation, the highest white birth rate at 2.2 children per woman[30], and natural resources galore. South Dakota suffers from abysmal homeschool regulations, encroaching liberalism from Illinois, Iowa, and Minnesota, and a rapidly growing Hispanic population. South Dakota is one of the better states on this list.

6. New Mexico

New Mexico is basically Mexico. Hey, at least real estate is ridiculously cheap, and the LLC privacy laws are good. 29 of New Mexico's sheriffs signed a statement against the ominous "red flag" gun confiscation laws being pushed by liberals nationwide[31]. It can't be all bad, can it?

7. Idaho

Business Insider provides critical insight on Idaho:

"...frustrated locals feel that the Californians are driving up prices. The cost of a typical home in Ada County, which includes Boise, hit nearly $300,000 in September, an 18%

---

[29] https://wallethub.com/edu/states-with-highest-lowest-tax-burden/20494/
[30] https://www.breitbart.com/politics/2019/01/13/states-birth-rate-2017/
[31] https://www.breitbart.com/2nd-amendment/2019/02/10/29-new-mexicos-33-sheriffs-sign-statement-against-red-flag-laws/

jump from the previous year, Gopal and Buhayar reported. One new gated community sells homes with huge windows and "wine walls" to mostly out-of-state buyers, a sales agent told the news outlet. The economic relief of moving to a down-home city is just one reason Idaho experienced a rise in popularity among Californians, who made up 85% of the state's total domestic immigration in 2016, Bloomberg reported, citing an analysis of US census data.[32"]

While an attractive option with inexpensive real estate outside of Boise, high white birthrates, no homeschool or vaccination regulations, the 10th lowest tax burden, and an electorate that leans heavily to the right, Boise has become a blight upon the state with a massive influx of liberals and their Third World white guilt accessories (non-white people). Idaho is poised to become the next Oregon, though Montana is giving it a run for its money. Longstanding middle-class prepper areas like the Idaho panhandle are ever more turning into tourist attractions featuring more and more Asians who have tired of going to Yellowstone. These challenges aside, Idaho is one of the better states on this list - especially if she can convince Boise to become a city state when the country breaks apart.

8. Nebraska

Nebraska features affordable real estate, a developed economy helmed by Omaha, an expansive western portion perfectly encapsulating the "fly over state" meme so loathed by America's coastal liberals, and a healthy white birth rate. Nebraska is a less free South Dakota with more productive farmers and cheaper real estate but more urbanism. Parts of Omaha and Council Bluffs on the other

---

[32] https://www.businessinsider.com/californians-priced-out-move-to-idaho-2018-10

side of the state line have been ghettoized and left to the wolves. Nebraska homeschool laws require annual notification to the school district and state mandated subjects[33].

9. Nevada

Las Vegas has the distinction of being the only city I've had a gun waved at me by a gangbanger. The city is fully multicultural and has the same political effect on the rest of the state that Portland has on Oregon or Boise has on Idaho. Nevada has long been a favorite of survivalist types due to its remoteness and extremely low population density outside of Reno and Las Vegas. Steel reinforced concrete fortresses such as the 8,000 square foot Hard Luck Castle in the tiny town of Gold Point, Nevada[34] are more commonly available than one would think. The state benefits from decent homeschool regulations, affordable real estate, remoteness, and plenty of sunshine. However, the state is becoming rapidly Mexicanized entirely throughout and longstanding survivalists are looking to move elsewhere. Nevada also has the distinction of being a high human trafficking state[35]. Nevada was once a southwestern paradise, but demographics have hamstrung the state.

10. Kansas

---

[33] https://projects.propublica.org/graphics/homeschool
[34] https://www.dailymail.co.uk/news/article-6634479/Fortress-middle-desert-three-hours-away-Las-Vegas-goes-sale-950-000.html
[35] https://www.insidermonkey.com/blog/11-worst-states-for-human-trafficking-in-america-524251/?singlepage=1

Kansas is similar to Nebraska but with much better homeschool laws, more insane weather, and a considerably lower white birthrate. The state has rapidly Mexicanized with parts of Topeka resembling the Hispanic favelas south of the US border. Real estate is affordable, there is no traffic even around the University of Kansas in the heart of 'KCK", and the people are Midwestern friendly. Some pluses, especially considering the prevalence of former nuclear silos turned into doomsday redoubts, but the state isn't quite as desirable as North or South Dakota.

Other interesting options for a stateside getaway include:

Vermont - high white population, affordable real estate, surprisingly low tax burden on lower/middle class folks, mountainous, statewide high-quality Internet, and situated at the forgotten end of New York state. Unfortunately, Vermonters are into killing babies, "The House approved H-0057 by a 106-36 vote. The bill allows women to abort a baby at any time and for any reason up until birth.[36]"

Maine - high white population, supremely affordable real estate, similar tax situation as Vermont, cold as Antarctica, the potential to Balkanize away into Canada's maritime provinces, and robust Food Freedom laws. Downside is that Portland is a Somali city, through and through.

West Virginia - whitest population in the Union, Third Worlders have a hard time assimilating due the distinct culture and already longstanding over usage of welfare by the local population, mountainous, rock bottom cheap real estate, decent Internet

---

[36] https://www.infowars.com/vt-house-passes-bill-legalizing-elective-abortions-until-birth/

propagation, and homeschool laws that are surprisingly lax despite the state's low ranking in homeschool freedom.

The possibility of moving overseas also exists. The consensus seems to be that the following countries are the most workable:

-Chile
-Uruguay
-Argentina
-St. Kitts and Nevis
-Japan
-Thailand
-Vietnam
-South Korea
-Singapore
-Hong Kong
-Poland
-Hungary
-Estonia
-Ukraine
-Slovakia

International relocation comes with its own set of problems such as visa complications, banking, socialization, and free speech limitations.

As America declines, strategic relocation should only be seen as a half-measure. There may be a few places that are better than others but the whole of America is bound by federal law, which ensures mass migration and multiculturalism at the point of a gun entirely throughout. Moving around during the decline is a speculative choice that may or may not lead to greater freedom in future generations. Strategic relocation can also act as a huge distraction from organizing other components of one's life during the decline or taking a stand and fighting for freedom within a liberal state. However, "stand and fight" can also be a sentimental folly that leads to worse outcomes than dealing with the uncertainty of living with a diaspora mindset. Whether whites, who have not practiced white identity until recently, are able to legally ensure their own continued survival remains yet to be seen. Strategic relocation does nothing to change the attitudes of the locals toward white preservationism. Building community, getting involved, and spreading the values of freedom and Western Civilization are all good strategies to place alongside or perhaps above strategic relocation. As Stefan Molyneux has said in response to people asking him what they can do about living in London and watching in horror at the rapid decline,

> "I wish I could tell you (what to do). Have some babies, speak the truth, and predict what's coming. To take an unrelated example from history. Churchill was in the wilderness. Churchill, after the mess at Gallipoli where he lost his admiralty and ended back at the trenches of the First World War, he was in the wilderness - considered an eccentric, a crazy. He was nuts but he predicted the rise of Hitler and coming of war. Just taking the standard narrative: It was Chamberlain who said, 'I've got peace in our time. Hitler is someone I can negotiate with, someone I can reason with,' and so on. Churchill is saying, 'No, he's an adventurer of the old school type. He's going to bring war. He's going to bring chaos. He's not kidding when he talks about the Jews.' And people are like, 'Yay, Chamberlain! Churchill's the worst guy ever. Patooey, patooey, patooey.' And then when people are cornered and desperate and realize there's no way out - then

they'll switch from Chamberlain to Churchill pretty quickly. People switch from the parliament in Chile to Augustus Pinochet pretty quickly. When people are desperate, they can change their minds pretty quickly, but you have to have been making the presentations. You have to be making the presentations to be right about your predictions."

While Molyneux's read on the facts of history is up for debate, his reading of the lessons of the official narrative is indisputable. America is facing a demographic cliff, but Brazil has gone over the cliff, at 48.43% of the population being white in 2008[37]. Brazil recently elected Jair Bolsonaro, a fiery leader whose rhetoric and talking points far outstrip the urgency of Donald J. Trump's platform. All hope is not lost.

The Germans in WWII were defeated by their own overextension and because they were bested by British intelligence, who cracked the Enigma code and proceeded to eviscerate German supply lines for the duration of the conflict. Intelligence and low time preference ruled the roost. Had Hitler been less impulsive in invading Poland, he could have taken more time to negotiate with the enemies that were encircling him. He could have achieved some degree of Lebensraum while keeping France and England off of his back. Instead he plunged in with false flags and promises of German glory. The ability to read into social and historical trends and emerge with a reasonably accurate picture of what will happen only bolsters a person's credibility. Hitler accurately predicted the Soviet menace but did not curtail his own ego in order to respond reasonably to the Soviet mortal threat. Hitler was too self-absorbed to have the

---

[37] https://en.wikipedia.org/wiki/Brazil#Race_and_ethnicity

predictive power that would leave a lasting positive effect on audiences of the era. The world carried on without him.

An accurate reading on the decline is critical for reversing the trends. Strategic relocation is no replacement for having difficult conversations with one's own family members. Have a parent who voted for Hillary Clinton and plans to vote for the NPR or CNN approved candidate in 2020? Maybe, just maybe they are putting the future of your children or unborn children at risk. Perhaps this needs to be patiently and kindly explained to them in terms they can understand. Or perhaps you have a younger person in the family, like a cousin, niece, or nephew, who would open to and be receptive of the message of freedom. Young people are idealistic and love to have causes. What better cause than the preservation and resurgence of Western Civilization once the globalists are unseated? Obviously, young people need mentoring in career related matters, and never should their philosophical beliefs put at risk their financial status before they are established. Yet, public schooling has done them no favors, leaving them wholly unprepared for what is coming. Nor does employment with a major corporation give them any philosophical bearing. Someone has to up their power levels and allow them to plan for the future that is sure to come. Who better than you, reader? Everyone needs someone to redpill them.

If you could warn Christians in the Holodomor of their impending slaughter by a Jewish-Soviet cabal, would you? If you could warn whites living in segregated neighborhoods in Arizona of their political dispossession and eventual physical displacement by Mexican cartel violence, would you? If you could warn African-American blacks living in Detroit of the globalist elite plan to replace them with a lower IQ Syrian Muslim population, would you[38]?

---

[38] https://www.breitbart.com/politics/2016/08/29/bill-clinton-calls-for-rebuilding-detroit-with-syrian-refugees/

Everyone reading has an audience they can reach and lives they can personally influence. All it takes is the courage to speak out. This is what can be done to prepare for the decline. The tides of history can change, and people will look to credible leadership. Who will sound out the alarm?

Mass Migration and Cultural Decline

Since demographic data has been tracked, the USA's birthrate peaked somewhere around the late 1950's at 3.65 children per mother[39]. The Baby Boom still echoes to this day. You can still find a burger joint or a malt shop in nearly every town across the country. The "oldies" still have a presence on FM radio. Baby Boomers shaped America into the consumer society it is today, and they hold major sway on Federal elections - vaulting one Donald J. Trump (born 1946) into the Presidency. Baby Boomers will continue to dominate the fiscal, electoral, and cultural landscape until they begin dying off in large numbers in the 2030's.

The top song of early 2019 is Ariana Grande's "7 rings", featuring the lyrics:

> "Wearing a ring, but ain't gon' be no "Mrs. Bought matching diamonds for six of my bitches. I'd rather spoil all my friends with my riches. Think retail therapy my new addiction."

Ariana's music video features a teenaged looking Ariana dressed like an absolute whore with a gaggle of whores behind her, writhing and wiggling with a pink motif dominating the entire scene. Most of the women are non-white and there are no men in any of the scenes. Certain scenes in the music video appear to be Satanic in nature with Ariana wearing goat ears and women in full body latex suits in the form of rabbits with neon half-moon lights nearby. Pink has been used by abortion advocacy groups to push for late term infanticide. The One World Trade Center was lit pink only a week ago in celebration of the legalization of abortion until birth in New York

---

[39] https://data.worldbank.org/indicator/SP.DYN.TFRT.IN

state[40]. Ariana, who comes from lower intelligence Italian parents who separated when she was around 8 or 9 years old[41], was caught on video saying, "I hate America, I hate Americans[42]." Her estimated net worth ranges from $45 million to $50 million, depending on the source[43]. Much of Ariana's audience is Hispanic, as she is commonly mistaken for a Hispanic, but she also draws from the hip-hop market with frequent collaborations and her own hip-hop vocals. In 2019 the most popular music genre is hip-hop at 25% share of the music sales market. Hispanic music charts in at fifth place with 9.4% and is now more popular than country music[44].

The top song of 1959 was Johnny Horton's "The Battle of New Orleans" featuring the lyrics,

> "In 1814 we took a little trip. Along with Colonel Jackson down the mighty Mississip. We took a little bacon and we took a little beans and we caught the bloody British in the town of New Orleans."

The music video features Horton dressed in Civil War attire, calmly holding a dated rifle, well-dressed young girls sitting in audience clapping as if they were on a school trip, and two variety show hosts dancing briefly. Clearly, Horton is lip synching on some early television show. Horton came from an Anglo-Saxon, English

---

[40] https://www.lifesitenews.com/news/new-york-celebrates-legalizing-abortion-until-birth-by-lighting-one-world-t
[41] https://www.billboard.com/articles/news/6221482/billboard-cover-ariana-grande-on-fame-freddy-krueger-and-her-freaky-past
[42] https://www.latimes.com/entertainment/gossip/83951108-157.html
[43] https://www.celebritynetworth.com/richest-celebrities/actors/ariana-grande-net-worth/
[44] https://www.forbes.com/sites/jeffbenjamin/2019/01/04/latin-music-in-2018-album-song-sales-consumption-buzzangle-report/#55a382ea5add

background. Horton was divorced once, married the widow of Hank Williams, and died in a car crash in 1960.

There is a cultural chasm between Ariana Grande and Johnny Horton. Mass migration and the resulting drop in global IQ[45] are most certainly culprits in this degeneration. White birthrate also has something do with it. The non-Hispanic white population share of the United States is somewhere around 62%. In 1959 this number was 85.4%. Hispanic share of the population was 3.2% in 1960 and 16.3% in 2010[46]. The white, non-Hispanic, birthrate sits at 1.6665 children per woman in America. It was 3.65 in 1957.

Digging into the IQ component briefly, the non-Hispanic white IQ is 97 (100 for Northern and Western Europeans). Hispanics clock in at 88 or 89[47]. This is nearly a standard of deviation difference. Research shows that countries with an average IQ below 90 fail to create or maintain democracy. America is undoubtedly becoming more Hispanic, especially Mexican. The average IQ of Mexico is 88 and Mexican political elites use mass migration to the United States as a dumping ground for their unwanted. The Mexicans coming over the southern border are lower than 88 IQ.

Ariana Grande has not come to prominence in an exciting new industry, mass media, to a population that is 39% rural[48] comprised of higher intelligence whites almost totally unencumbered by any welfare programs. She has come to prominence in an aged industry that keeps out dissident voices to a population that is 19.3%

---

[45] https://www.fourmilab.ch/documents/IQ/1950-2050/

[46] https://en.wikipedia.org/wiki/Historical_racial_and_ethnic_demographics_of_the_United_States

[47] https://aristocratsofthesoul.com/average-iq-by-race-and-ethnicity/

[48] https://www2.census.gov/library/publications/1959/compendia/statab/80ed/1959-02.pdf?#

rural[49] (all population growth in the United States has been urban since WWII) to an increasingly mixed-race population with dropping IQ figures and welfare programs estimated to total more than $1,091 billion as of 2011.

Social capital, a measure of the wellness of communities in a society, has been on a severe decline since around 1965[50]. The states with the highest remaining social capital are all highly tilted toward European ethnic homogeneity.

With these factors in mind, we have gutter music as the cultural jewel of the United States. No longer are our most popular songs from the folk or traditional country genres. We are no longer told stories of American heroes like Andrew Jackson defending the sovereignty of the nation. Our concert-goers are no longer seated in an opry, dressed tastefully and using the music to connect with others in a sober fashion.

The gutter music broadcast through our nation by groups with no loyalty to the United States or any love for white people features themes of early sexual promiscuity, feminism, materialism, and occult symbology. In 1959, music was for families to enjoy and lyrical content was highly monitored to ensure wholesome, Christian compliance. 60 years later the music is written by teams of 8 to 20 engineers and liberal propagandists to ensure massive capture of youth markets. Music and music videos are being scientifically engineered to have maximum impact on the developing brains of children[51]. There is no focus on the family. The family structure is

---

[49] https://www.census.gov/newsroom/press-releases/2016/cb16-210.html
[50] Putnam RD. Bowling Alone: The Collapse and Revival of American Community. New York: Simon & Schuster; 2000.
[51] https://curiosity.com/topics/this-song-was-carefully-engineered-to-make-babies-happy-curiosity/

discouraged for all heterosexuals. Only non-heterosexuals may raise children but only if the children are raised to become non-heterosexuals themselves. Sexuality has become a battering ram plowing into the subconscious minds of children. Once their boundaries are obliterated, they are injected with nihilism and a hatred for white males.

The culture of 2019 is a gutter because Westerners decided they should sell out their future generations for welfare entitlements in the here and now. Unfunded liabilities (mostly Social Security and Medicare promises) totaling $100 trillion will ensure that Millennials, Zoomers, and the generation after Zoomers (some call them Generation Alpha) will never see the economic prosperity that Boomers saw in the 1950's, 1960's, and parts of the following three decades. To paraphrase popular radio personality and broadcaster Anthony Cumia, "Boomers sold out their children and grandchildren for guaranteed dental into old age."

The culture will not recover until the moral argument for smaller government (or no government at all) is successfully embedded in the minds of the majority of the voting population. With the current non-Hispanic white share of the hospital births in 2019 hovering around 49.8%[52], this will be a tall order. Non-whites, including Jews, simply do not vote for smaller government[53]. Nor do these trends operate in a vacuum, given the mass invasion of the West by Third World peoples.

The top 100 on the Billboard charts make sense, given the population. Spurred on by free welfare handouts, Third Worlders are breeding at much higher rates than native whites. The music

---

[52] http://www.pewresearch.org/fact-tank/2016/06/23/its-official-minority-babies-are-the-majority-among-the-nations-infants-but-only-just/
[53] http://www.pewresearch.org/fact-tank/2018/11/08/the-2018-midterm-vote-divisions-by-race-gender-education/

promotes sexual cultures from countries with consent laws as low as 12. The lyrical content averages a 2.6 grade reading level[54] and will only continue to trend downwards. The Third World was depleted of its most competence, intelligence, and industrious peoples early on in the mass migration program instituted by the 1965 Immigration Act. The people who are coming now bring long eradicated diseases, genital mutilation practices, gang affiliations, and rape cultures. These people have cultural needs and who better than Ariana Grande to meet those needs?

Songs like "7 rings" exist because the excesses of the West are not invested in the future. The Golden Generation kicked this off by trusting Lyndon Johnson and Ted Kennedy with immigration policy. The Boomers continued the trend with furthered lowering of immigration restrictions, mass amnesties, and popular support for Israeli proxy wars in the Middle East. Millennials, in their apathy and overstimulation, give little hope to the cause of liberty by retaining the title of "most liberal age group"[55]. The apathy, white guilt, and distractions will have to end before a beautiful, family-oriented culture can be reinstituted. Unfortunately, most Americans have been and will continue to be happy to live off the excesses of post-WWII America until the bill comes due. Most people only learn through social cataclysm. The political elite know this well and are extending the lifespan of this sick governmental system as long as possible while they make their preparations. The gig is only up when The Machine can no longer dazzle the masses with CGI movies helmed by child

---

[54] https://www.buzzfeed.com/javiermoreno/third-graders-write-better-lyrics
[55] http://www.pewresearch.org/fact-tank/2014/09/25/the-gops-millennial-problem-runs-deep/

rapists[56] and pubescent pop stars stoking up child rape fantasies implanted by the feminist mass media.

---

[56] https://www.polygon.com/2019/1/24/18196562/bryan-singer-red-sonja-sexual-misconduct

Junk In, Junk Out

"The unconscious is the true accumulation of your history. It can be accepted or rejected but it can't fundamentally be altered."

-Stefan Molyneux

There was a secret order in Germany in the mid-18th century that called itself the Great Enlightened Society of Oculists. From Wired Magazine, "...the Oculists fixated on both the anatomy and symbolism of the eye. They focused on sight as a metaphor for knowledge.[57]" The Oculists closely guarded what their eyes beheld as they believed that what the eye takes in has tremendous power over the mind[58]. Anyone who has used social media for any amount of time has experienced firsthand the dizzying, whack-a-mole effect it has on one's own ability to concentrate. Smart phones dumb people down by disrupting their ability to focus on concepts for an extended period of time. Combine this disrupting effect with profane imagery and the net effect on a person's consciousness is more akin to a circus than a Grecian library of antiquity. Junk in, junk out, as the old saying goes.

Let's have fun with this.

The Oculists were on to something. The media has become rife with occult symbology. Viewers are regularly exposed to bizarre new age moments in car commercials, cinema with deeply embedded anti-white assumptions, and pornographic pop stars who do strange

---

[57] https://www.wired.com/2012/11/ff-the-manuscript/
[58] https://www.youtube.com/watch?v=Ub-OP8NFPGM

things like cover one of their eyes or dance in front of pyramids capped by all-seeing eyes. The symbology is meant to elicit certain reactions and form certain ideas for the viewers. While deciphering the depths of occult symbology for its meaning is probably not be the most productive use of time, even a cursory reading of Jungian psychology will reveal to a reader the importance of symbols throughout human history[59].

On a recent broadcast of his titled, "Is watching the UFC a homosexual act?[60]" comedian Owen Benjamin discussed at length the imagery employed by the UFC. While partly in jest, Owen's original comedic demeanor eventually gave way to a serious consideration of the question. Owen cited an image of two male fighters pressing their faces together, including their lips, to the delight of UFC President Dana White in the background as evidence of a homosexual agenda on the part of the UFC. Owen also discussed the idea that men gather in groups to watch the UFC's pay-per-view broadcasts out of a vicarious desire to "get physical" with other men in a manner that would be sexually stimulating. I would argue that the UFC preys upon Western man's desire to sublimate his violent impulses in order to keep him from organizing outside the system. Same goes for the NFL, NBA, and so forth.

The point being, by focusing on faraway men (sometimes in sexual positions) hitting each other, the male viewer never encodes into his unconscious the lived experience of combat or even physical competition. In a very real sense, watching sports only begets more watching sports. The lived experience is one of passive spectating, not thrilling competition. The viewer willingly relinquishes his physical

---

[59] Neumann, E. (2014). The origins and history of consciousness. With a foreword by C.G. Jung. Lawrenceville: Princeton University Press.
[60] https://www.youtube.com/watch?v=TQWIrcAddBc

potential to the athlete on the screen. This is kind of gay. Certainly, it's domesticated behavior.

Another example of passive viewing having a homosexualizing effect can be found in Internet pornography. The viewer of Internet pornography masturbates to the image of another man having sex with a woman. He is cuckolding himself the way a pre-television era man only could by watching a man sleep with his wife or watch a man sleep with a prostitute he hired. This is also kind of gay.

The imagery a person projects out into the world is an aesthetic reflection of his unconscious. Others take on this imagery as passive consumers and encode the imagery into their personality, as it is their lived experience for however long they viewed the material. To torture and eventually break the mind of a prisoner, a captor may expose the prisoner to video footage on a loop of the prisoner's loved ones being tortured and raped. Or the captor may use violent pornography or some innocuously repetitive pop song for hours and days on end. The prisoner's mind breaks, and compliance is attained.

The horror of modernity is that people willingly break their own minds all the time in all corners of the globe where mass media has proliferated. People willingly flood themselves with imagery to the point of overwhelm, on a daily and continual basis. Social media speeds up this process. Of course, not all mass media is occultic symbology or pornographic. But a great deal of it is. Junk in, junk out.

The Catholic Church understood the power of imagery and went to great lengths to ensure the iconographic veneration of Jesus Christ. Profane imagery that aped and mocked Jesus was banned. Pornography was banned. Painters were commissioned to depict scenes that would further the narratives of the Church. The civilization wreckers who took the helm of mass media in the 20th century immediately set about to completely destroy the iconographic power of the Church and uncouple the deep, unconscious narratives of man from the virtue of divinity. Nuns in orgies were depicted. Jesus was depicted as a woman or a black man. Idiotic consumers were all too happy to join in the frenzy. The Boomer generation lavished untold fortunes onto media moguls like the Weinsteins, Spielberg, Geffen, and others who were all too happy to present audiences with smut and false depictions of history. Presently the image creators and distributors no longer have to contend with the iconographic power of the Church. They have free license to depict little women beating up hulking men, all manner of sexual perversions, cartoon characters fighting for social justice, and so forth. The largest film franchise in Hollywood is helmed by James Gunn, a pedophile who posted things to Twitter such as, "The Expendables was so manly I fucked the shit out of the little pussy boy next to me! The boys ARE back in town!" He was reinstated in early 2019 by Disney months after a successful boycott was led against him by Mike Cernovich and others.

The deluge of imagery unleashed by the civilization wreckers is meant to overwhelm, paralyze, and infect audiences with myths and sentimentality that will reinforce the coming of a global government. People are all too happy to give their attention and money to these "imagineers", especially the Third World and emerging markets such as China. The Chinese maintain a fascistic control on their cinema industry, up until recent years only allowing 10 foreign films screened in the country per year. The Chinese government has ensured the themes and imagery in their cinema reinforce the ruling power of the ruling party. Foreign film studios are willing to go to great lengths to screen their films in the emerging market, even editing portions of their films or putting Chinese characters in more prominent positions.

The doctrine of social equality is the main myth of modern media. Equality is pushed so that whites are dispossessed and willingly dispossess themselves. Gun control is pushed with the removal of firearms from the films of The Rock in favor of effeminate rope swinging and gap jumping. Interracial couples are the norm, despite their statistical minority in reality. Homosexuality is the new heterosexuality. Whites are always and forever the dolts and bad guys. Blacks are brilliant scientists far and away more often than whites. Hispanics are always aggrieved and worthy of compassion as they struggle to illegally cross America's southern border and never are they shown to consume the massive amounts of welfare they do. The peacefulness of migrants, compared to US natives, is forever on display - never mind the lack of adjustment for race on the part of US natives. Superheroes always fight angry white males. Transsexuals are depicted as joyful and wise, despite their record-breaking levels of suicide. The German Nazis are completely and totally depicted as Satanic psychopaths lacking even a microscopic bit of humanity. The Holocaust is the most important thing that ever happened ever, and it should never be forgotten even for a single hour by anyone anywhere always. People from disparate groups get along just fine and always overcome evil whitey. Furry cartoon animals are shown doing drugs and being smashed to pieces helter-skelter in a slapstick fashion. The Manhattan dating scene takes precedence over family values. Every mentally incapacitated minority who ever won a ribbon of some kind must have their life's story made into a 2-hour Netflix movie. Promiscuity is more common than drinking water. Christians are weak and stupid while Islam is dignified and powerful.

The inversion of values into psychotic madness never ends. That's the whole point. Only when all of the joy and meaning is sucked out of life can a person truly capitulate to the aims of the global elite. The lower the IQ and the worse the childhood, the easier it is to finish a person off with sick imagery. The great mass of humanity is relatively self-unaware and almost totally susceptible to unconscious programming.

This is why it is so important to be judicious with the imagery you take in and to limit passive consumption of media. Even the highest-flying business executive sees his most productive hours of the day limited to three[61]. People too often give their three best hours of the day over to media executives who program them with degenerate, Satanic, and globalist messages! This is a colonization of the mind. People are not living their own lives. They are living according to the needs of the global elite broadcasting their myths out into the world.

Getting out of this mess involves reasserting the importance the unconscious. The person on their deathbed whose head is filled with all the TV shows they watched throughout their lives instead of memories of flesh and blood experience is a person who utterly failed in this regard. There are too many dead people walking. Too much junk in the trunk! The solution is to pay careful attention to the types of messages, images, and sounds a person consumes from media. Better to know the songs of an obscure folk band than the repetitive, sentimental lyrics of the British intelligence service backed The Beatles. Better to have watched some philosopher in an empty room talking about the importance of self-knowledge for ten hours than devoting ten hours to an Amazon mini-series about lesbian journalists under attack by the patriarchy. Better to know the soaring, angelic heights of a Raphael painting than the dull, annoying quips of the Cards Against Humanity game. Better to simply forgo screens altogether in order to spend time with friends, family, and nature. For many this involves overcoming the fear of missing out. People want to

---

[61] https://www.inc.com/melanie-curtin/in-an-8-hour-day-the-average-worker-is-productive-for-this-many-hours.html

stay glued to their devices because they want to be "in the know" on the latest. This is a way of feeling personally efficacious in the face of far-off world events that are largely outside of a person's power to influence.

Our sense of sight is the most dominant of the five senses. Second comes our sense of hearing. The civilization wreckers know this and program their media accordingly. It is hard to communicate Communism through touch without murdering millions of people. Better to make a dazzling display of Communism than to make people taste it through the metallic, gunpowder flavor of the barrel of a gun or dust in the mouth from a widespread famine. Imagery is easy. It slides right into the mind, accepted without resistance by the eyes.

We must offer healthy, even divine imagery. We must wed our ideals to beauty, order, harmony, and tranquility. The magnificent murals of Christianity depicting Heaven and the Creator must be improved upon, if possible. Glamor must be reined in to serve the purposes of family and community. The entire aesthetic of current commercial output must be redone. As those who control these institutions will not cede without a terrible fight, we must find alternative audiences and sources of funding in order to match their production values. We need our own "The Rock" driving a spear into the heart of the Devil as St. Michael once did in Scripture. Or better yet, shooting the Devil from a distance with a sniper rifle! Why not? We're having fun with this. We need imagery of interventions in child abuse. We need to see scenes of fertile mothers cradling their children while sitting in fields of wildflowers. We need to see images of rebels scaling the walls of elite compounds to make arrests on civilization wreckers. We need to see adults dissuading the youth from sexual perversions and guiding them to wholesome relationships. We need to see realistic depictions of space travel.

We must bring to life our imagination of what the very best of humanity is capable of. We have the ability to be "imagineers" for a new generation.

Domestication

> "I think the real reason so many youngsters are clamoring for freedom of some vague sort, is because of unrest and dissatisfaction with present conditions; I don't believe this machine age gives full satisfaction in a spiritual way, if the term may be allowed."
>
> -Robert E. Howard

With cultural Marxism taking advantage of female evil, society has become increasingly effeminized. Women gained the vote and immediately instituted social welfare programs. Voting went from a men's club of propertied politicians known for their masculine appeal to our modern-day soup of victimhood candidates sweeping into office from the ghetto on the strength of their anti-heterosexual-white-male rhetoric. White Christian men, long renowned as the kindest of all to their women, let female nagging get to them. As a result, America is swiftly becoming a boundaryless free for all.

One look at the effeminized landscape and you will see such sights as a Vegan Gay Men's group in Portland, Oregon. They dub themselves the Soyboys, "Soyboys is a local group of vegan gay men who host dine-outs and attend special events throughout the city. We love visiting the best vegan and veg-friendly spots around the city." They exclude meat-eaters, "Members can be vegan, vegetarian, or veg-curious gay men." In a city whose unofficial motto is *Keep Portland Weird* there is little to no chance any sort of legal pressure will be put on the group to do away with their discriminatory standards. The more non hetero-normative you are, the more you can operate out in the open without legal repercussions.

The long climb back to cultural and political hegemony for the straight white male is well documented on message boards like 4chan.org and on right wing social media. Values are so inverted in America that meritocracy is shouted down by the gatekeepers and other "influencers". White males built the West and despite higher IQ scores from Asians and Jews, whites are almost entirely responsible for the major scientific advances of the past 500 years. People from Western countries account for 83% of all Nobel laureates ever[62]. Of course, this will change as the Nobel Prize organization bows to the anti-meritocratic pressures of liberal identity politics. Nobel Prizes will eventually be given out to female-to-male transsexuals who dabble in science labs from time to time. The people doing the awarding will be proud Latinx women who, in their private lives, are accustomed to screaming and shouting to get their way. White men, so ready to pour forth engineers, philosophers, and learned-adventurers, in an effort to engage in interstellar exploration if left to their own devices, must now accept their economic, cultural, and political displacement so that envious stupid people and nagging women can feel secure in themselves.

This is occurring despite native born American white males being the only group statistically proven to be keeping alive the institution of free speech and the push for smaller government in the West[63]. Civilization is hanging by a thread.

---

[62] https://io9.gizmodo.com/this-map-of-nobel-prize-winners-shows-a-disturbing-leve-1446346273

[63] https://www.youtube.com/watch?v=rC2xU_efdzU&feature=youtu.be

Domestication has occurred on a mass scale since the World Wars. Western men were tricked into slaughtering one another by a certain political elite. Without understanding the true nature of these wars, the West has been sickened with guilt. The guilt quickly turned into nihilism. And Communists in the hundreds of thousands spread along the face of this expanding apathy like skilled ice skaters, all too happy to flaunt their sick message as they went along. Without a moral indictment of the elites who led the West into war, Western man has turned to consumption and self-domestication to try and cope. Why follow any more "strong men" when they led everyone into mindless slaughter? Better to adhere to the television and idolize non-political athletes. But even that source of comfort is gone as the athletes[64] have become social activists eager to advance the liberal agenda. Video games, the underground of male achievement, have been co-opted by politically correct corporations. Cinema is no better, with pedophiles helming the major hits of the day. The top film of 2019 is Captain Marvel starring Brie Larson, who has said, "I don't need a 40-year-old white dude to tell me what didn't work about A Wrinkle in Time. It wasn't made for him! I want to know what it meant to women of color, biracial women, to teen women of color.[65]" Of course, Brie Larson is ideological and blinded to the systemic racism against white men inherent in the film industry. White man has nowhere left to live vicariously. Even porn is riddled with Jewish directors pairing white women with black men or making every story line between whites about incest. Good riddance to porn, anyway.

---

[64] https://www.independent.co.uk/news/world/americas/us-politics/taking-a-knee-national-anthem-nfl-trump-why-meaning-origins-racism-us-colin-kaepernick-a8521741.html
[65] https://www.louderwithcrowder.com/brie-larson-i-dont-want-to-hear-what-a-white-man-has-to-say/

The domestication is complete. According to a UN report, 1 in 10 men in the United States get vasectomies. That rate triples for men in Canada and quintuples for men in the UK[66]. There is a 30% increase in vasectomy rates just prior to the NCAA basketball tournament[67], as the viewing experience allows for plenty of recovery time for men.

Consumer credit has played a massive part in the domestication of white men. Whites have the highest credit card debt rates of all the races in the United States at $6500 per person yet they have the lowest rate of credit card debt ownership at 42.1%[68].

Race	Debt	% with Debt
White	$6,500	42.1%
Black	$3,800	47.8%
Hispanic	$3,800	49.6%
Other	$5,700	44.1%

Generation	Age	Debt
Silent Generation	age 72+	$4,613
Baby Boomers	age 54-72	$7,550
Generation X	age 38-53	$7,750

---

[66] http://www.un.org/en/development/desa/population/publications/pdf/family/trendsContraceptiveUse2015Report.pdf
[67] http://fortune.com/2017/03/16/vasectomies-%20during-march-madness/?xid=time_socialflow_%20twitter
[68] https://www.creditdonkey.com/average-credit-card-debt.html

Generation Y	age 24-38	$4,315
Generation Z	age <24	$2,047

The younger generations (Gen-X, Millennials, and Zoomers) have the highest amount of revolving credit card usage as credit cards have simply become a fact of life. Consumer credit shields people from the negative social consequences of their bad behavior. There is no more saving for a rainy day and there hasn't been since the Silent Generation. Unwanted pregnancies are no longer catastrophic because the state offers welfare, and credit cards can buy up all the diapers a single mom needs. Keeping a job isn't as important when you can rack up $50,000 in credit card debt before the creditors start harassing you. Credit cards have gone from an "emergency only" use to a "spend now, pay later" ethos. Why not? The Boomers signed themselves up for $100 trillion in unfunded liabilities. What's it going to hurt to pile some consumer debt on top of that?

Debt is slavery. Slavery is sexy because of the slave morality of democracy. It's best to be on the bottom because that's the position from which a person can extract the most resources. Until automation sweeps in like the hurricane it will be, there is no consequence for debt or stupidity. In fact, these are values! The government and corporations encourage it. They know the final score. Their administrators and CEOs will be happily seated in their gated compounds as the world burns. The rest of us poor schmucks will live with no prospect of a better tomorrow as we're drowned in debt and swamped by lower IQ populations.

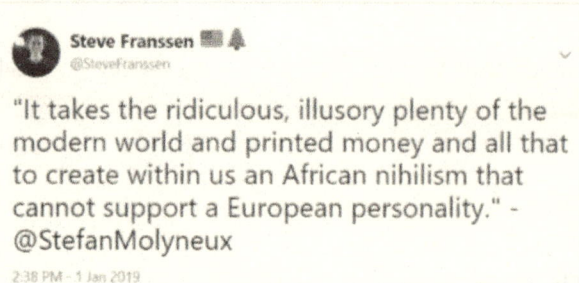

The domesticating nature of modern society is so pervasive that it can be referred to as "modernity". Everything lauded in the culture is sick and degenerate because the core is rotten. Western men sold the soul of their civilization out for central banking, women voting, the welfare system, and for allying with Communists to shatter the spine of Europe - the German people. Communism simply can't be morally indicted in the West because they were our greatest allies! Thankfully, we have a President in Trump who knows that you wait out tyrants like Hitler rather than sprint headlong into oblivion as Churchill did.

Western society has become soft. A whole host of white fellows with thick beards, their own podcast shows, and a penchant for lifting weights will tell you so. In a way, I'm throwing in with their lot. They're on to something, even if I have my critiques.

It's no mystery what white men need in today's day and age. They need the full and unabashed truth. No half measures. No manipulative warnings away from "the blandishments" of racial awareness. White men need to know how badly they shot themselves in the foot with the World Wars. White men need to know about the scientific studies showing the intelligence differences between the races[69] so they can understand how liberals have poisoned the minds of Third Worlders into thinking that inequalities in income always and forever stem from white bigotry, not inborn differences. With daily average media consumption at 506 minutes in 2017[70], white men need to learn the value of going out in nature and of lifting weights.

The time is well past to reject the domesticating and effeminizing forces at play in the West. Western man must remake himself. He must overcome female nagging, the identity politics of the left, vicarious entertainment, consumer credit, the impulses to rage and war, and the self-doubt that led him to sell out so fundamentally in the first place. In battling these evils, white man will reclaim his dignity and masculinity.

Let's get into the meat of this book and discuss what masculinity is and is not.

---

[69] Herrnstein, R. (1995). The Bell Curve. New York: Free Press.
[70] https://qz.com/416416/we-now-spend-more-than-eight-hours-a-day-consuming-media/

Masculinity and Parenting

"I am a more subtle alpha male because most of the alpha males around are chest-beating and driving around in sports cars and bagging models and the endless adolescence of people like Leonardo DiCaprio. They are considered to be the alpha males. That's not really an alpha male, that's a hedonist. A real alpha male is the person who influences culture and society significantly. I have convinced probably a hundred thousand families to stop hitting their children, I have convinced people to homeschool, I have convinced people to have children, I get regularly invitations to and photographs of people who got married because they met through philosophy and had conversations about values ahead of time. I know that I have significant influence in various political halls so, yes, as far as having an effect and influence on the world -which to me is the real definition of 'alpha' - yes. And because it's a positive influence it's alpha plus virtue."

-Stefan Molyneux

Masculinity is the biologically male roles and responsibilities which serve one's own biological children. Fatherhood and masculinity are inseparable. Masculinity works in confluence with fatherhood and cannot be divorced from fatherhood.

This conception of masculinity means that lots of the meaty posturing from self-proclaimed experts on the subject falls short of an ideal standard. For example, a man can lift the heaviest weights in the gym, smoke big cigars, boast six figure incomes, and sleep with pretty women but do these things out of a personal insecurity and avoidance of the responsibility of pair-bonding, marrying, and raising healthy children. Happens all the time. From the outside looking in, such a person leaves quite the impression. Inwardly he is still immature, and his purposes are skewed. He will attract vain, insecure audiences who wish to emulate him. Some of these people will pair bond, marry, and raise healthy children out of emulating such a man but it will have been their own commitment to propagating their kind that will distinguish them as masculine - not the fancy dressings of their guru.

A particularly strong example of masculinity comes to us from the novel *Growth of the Soil* by Knut Hamsun[71]. The novel tells the story of Isak, a Norwegian man who settles a plot of land some distance away from the nearest village. He is not a handsome or wealthy man. He has the work ethic of an ox. Work ethic is a critical component of masculinity. With his sheer working ability, he is able to raise some animals and attract a woman named Inger, who he has several children with. Throughout this novel Isak continually improves the lot of those around him through his dedication to work and his thrift, despite major disruptions and downright evil from the people who come into his sphere of influence. Isak sires an ambitious son and a workhorse son.

Isak deals with female evil in the most exemplary fashion: with absolute resolve without brutality. He takes no shortcuts. He leads by his humble example and endures incredible hardship without complaint. He tries his hand at prospects and investments but never gives up his core: his stellar work ethic. He does well by his children in the helping manner lauded by some of the best psychologists concerned with parenting. We'll get to that in a bit.

---

[71] Hamsun, K. (1921). Growth of the soil. New York: Knopf.

Also relevant is what Isak does *not* do. He does not use substances or drink to excess, sexualize his children, whimper and negotiate with female evil, boast or persuade, pretend he is a barbarian for living out in the woods, concern himself with the latest fashions, indulge in entertainment, marry outside of his community, get an education and constantly remind others where he got his degree from, fret over his hair, complain about his aches and pains, manipulate his children into normalizing any feelings of insecurity he may have, or commit adultery. In so many respects he is the Christian ideal. The novel is distrustful of the dissociating effects industrialization, modernization, and civilization has had on the Western personality. Isak is a vitalist, naturalist character. It is important to note that Norway has not given into the population replacement pressures of the globalist elite. Norwegians are happy with their nature and celebrate their rich culture openly. As a quarter Norwegian myself, I am all too happy to share in this proud heritage. The example of Isak is crucial for anyone looking to peel back the layers of pretense so often sold as solutions by foolish and manipulative people who have lost touch with their true Western roots. *Growth of the Soil* is a highly recommended read.

The Holy Bible offers a humble perspective in 1 Timothy 6:10 that is often forgotten in masculinity circles, "For the love of money is a root of all kinds of evils. It is through this craving that some have wandered away from the faith and pierced themselves with many pangs." While the acquisition of wealth and property is important to raising and providing for children, we have entered a brave new world where ostentatious displays of wealth have become the norm. The hip-hop lifestyle, which is anti-masculine and has everything to do with African nihilism, has penetrated deep into the heart of the West. Countless millions want to be "influencers" on social media and it's no secret that the quick path to success is to flaunt one's wealth. This attitude persists even among conservatives, who are supposed to be adhering to Christian principles they pay lip service to. The bucolic ideal that created actual wealth in America once infused the dealings of farmers and small businessmen. That has all been forgotten or deliberately discarded for the cosmopolitan ideal of materialism. There are some of the super wealthy that persist in the old ideals, but they don't make the tabloids or show their faces at publicity events. Their example isn't readily on display. While the so-called "King of Instagram" Dan Bilzerian may leave a considerable impression on his 25.9 million followers with an endless exhibition of scantily clad women adorned with breast implants and taking exotic outings all over the Third World, the price he paid long ago was the chance at being a genuine force for moral good in the world. Now he is a purveyor of smut, drugs, steroids, and the postmodern nihilism of the African personality. It's no surprise his profile picture is a Satanic image of a goat with long horns.

Money is an engine for choice. It is human labor quantified. A masculine man will employ money in the service of causes nobler than himself. He will donate to charity when appropriate, respond to market needs in an ethical manner, enrich the lives of himself and his loved ones with purpose and mission, and seek to ensure future generations will have the chance to work at higher-order problems than the problems he faced in his own day. A non-masculine man will only spread idolatry throughout the world.

Another strong example of masculinity can be found in the example of St. Michael the Archangel. *The Holy Bible*, Revelation 12:7-9, reads:

> "Fierce war broke out in heaven, where Michael and his angels fought against the dragon. The dragon and his angels fought on their part, but could not win the day, or stand their ground in heaven any longer; the great dragon, serpent of the

primal age, was flung down to earth; he whom we call the devil, or Satan, the whole world's seducer, flung down to earth, and his angels with him."

St. Michael gives the example of warring with evil, even at the risk of total annihilation, in order to ensure the future of all God's children. Depictions of St. Michael often portray him standing over Satan and his fallen angels, with a sword or spear in hand. As Michael Walsh writes, "Michael, the hyper-masculine commander of the Heavenly Host, is the archetype for every fearless warrior who's ever lived.[72]" St. Michael's ultimate resolve and killing power embody the Western ideal of moral righteousness so deeply lacking in white culture today. The vitality of masculine achievement in antiquity is forever captured by the St. Michael ideal.

As part of the ideal of fatherhood, masculinity entails the acquisition of space. Bronze Age Pervert writes:

> "A healthy animal not under distress, not maimed, not trapped by man, seeks first when young: space. Animals seek space in a physical sense, territory... Only after full development of its powers and its mastery over space specific to its needs does the need or desire for reproduction come.[73]"

A responsibility to serve one's own biological children entails mastery over a physical space. This paves the path for a successful, secure family life. This is true for all mammals. With foreign hordes staging a full-scale invasion, Western man has the impetus now more than ever to secure and master a space for the benefit of his children. This is a

---

[72] Walsh, M. (2018). The Fiery Angel: Art, Culture, Sex, Politics, and the Struggle for the Soul of the West. Encounter Books.
[73] Pervert, B. A. (2018). Bronze age mindset: An exhortation. San Bernardino, CA: Bronze Age Pervert.

painful prospect, given the artificially inflated real estate prices and lack of breadwinner jobs because of Boomers and regulators wrecking the economy. However, it must be done if a man wants his kids to have a secure future. Sure, children can be brought up in "rented space" and turn out decently but the ideal of owning space gives a man a vested interest in the future outcomes of his homeland. The man who fights for his people's place at the table fulfills this masculine ideal. He serves not only his own responsibilities as a father, he serves other moral men in his tribe in their quest to achieve a family friendly society. A man who is forced to pay property tax for all the stupid political inventions of the people around him learns quickly the attitudes and dispositions appropriate to a caretaker of space. Owning space is an ideal and not a reality for many men in the West. The system is rigged against property ownership.

Parenting is a critical component of masculinity. Whether a man parents well or not is a huge indicator of his worthiness and honor. Is his leadership style in the home that of a philosopher-king, scoundrel, tyrant, or couch potato? Is he absent or is he present?

Lloyd deMause, who founded the discipline of "psychohistory" in 1974, posited six modes of parenting he observed historically and across cultures[74]. The following is an overview from the Internet[75]:

> 1. Infanticidal - Ritual sacrifice. High infanticide rates, incest, body mutilation, child rape and tortures. (Author's note: Such parenting is still present in the least developed parts of the world, including the Amazon and parts of the Middle East

---

[74] deMause, Lloyd (January 1982). Foundations of Psychohistory. Creative Roots Publishing. pp. 61 & 132–146.
[75] https://en.wikipedia.org/wiki/Psychohistory

and Africa. Pre-Greek and Roman societies in the West were commonly of this mode.)

2. Abandoning - Infanticide replaced by abandonment. Those children who survived the experience did not internalize a completely murderous superego. Longer swaddling, fosterage, outside wet nursing, oblation of children to monasteries and nunneries, and apprenticeship. Routine pederasty of boys continued in monasteries and elsewhere, and the rape of girls was commonplace. (Note: Such parenting is routine in underdeveloped Africa, the Middle East, India, and parts of Asia.)

3. Ambivalent - The later Middle Ages ended abandonment of children to monasteries. Early beating, shorter swaddling, mourning for deceased children, a precursor to empathy. (Note: This mode of parenting is the standard of the Third World.)

4. Intrusive - During the 16th century, particularly in England, parents shifted from trying to stop children's growth to trying to control them and make them obedient. Parents were prepared to give them attention as long as they controlled their minds, their insides, their anger and the lives they led. The intrusive parent began to unswaddle the infant. Early toilet training, repression of child's sexuality. (Note: This is the mode of parenting in the most advanced parts of the Third World.)

5. Socializing - Beginning in the 18th century, mothers began to enjoy child care, and fathers began to participate in younger children's development. The aim remained instilling parental goals rather than encouraging individuation.

Manipulation and spanking were used to make children obedient. Hellfire and the harsher physical disciplinary actions using objects to beat the child disappeared. The Socializing Mode remains the most popular model of parenting in North America and Western Europe to the present day. Use of guilt, "mental discipline", humiliation, time-out, rise of compulsory schooling, delegation of parental unconscious wishes. As parental injections continued to diminish, the rearing of the child became less a process of conquering its will than of training it. The socializing psychoclass built the modern world.

6. Helping - Beginning in the mid-20th century, some parents adopted the role of helping children reach their own goals in life, rather than "socialize" them into fulfilling parental wishes. Less manipulation, more unconditional love. Children raised in this way are far more empathic towards others in society than earlier generations. This mode is marked by the children's rights movement (often subverted by Satanists), natural childbirth, the abandonment of circumcision, attachment parenting, Taking Children Seriously, unconditional parenting, Parent Effectiveness Training, deschooling and free schooling. (Note: This is the mode of parenting in the most advanced places in the West.)

deMause's overview of the Helping Mode from the original book clarifies:

"The helping mode involves the proposition that the child knows better than the parent what it needs at each stage of its life, and fully involves both parents in the child's life as they work to empathize with and fulfill its expanding and particular needs. There is no attempt at all to discipline or form 'habits'. Children are neither struck nor scolded and are apologized to if yelled at under stress. The helping mode involves an enormous amount of time, energy, and discussion on the part of both parents, especially in the first six years, for helping a young child reach its daily goals means continually responding to it, playing with it, tolerating its regressions, being its servant rather than the other way around, interpreting its emotional conflicts, and providing the objects specific to its evolving interests. Few parents have yet (as of 1982) consistently attempted this kind of child care. From the books which describe children brought up according to the helping mode, it is evident that it results in a child who is gentle, sincere, never depressed, never imitative or group-oriented, strong-willed, and unintimidated by authority."

I will posit a seventh mode of parenting: philosophical parenting. This mode of parenting is most commonly referred to as "peaceful parenting":

> 7. Peaceful Parenting - Beginning in the early 21st century, a rare few parents adopted the role of raising their children entirely without manipulation. Parental focus on imbuing or imparting self-sustaining virtue in their children. Children raised in this way are far more empathetic than those raised in the Helping mode as they are fully prepared to become moral, philosophical agents of change in adulthood. This mode is marked by parental self-knowledge and self-therapy, unconditional love with a future focus on standards of moral excellence in adulthood, attachment parenting, homeschooling, whole food diets with sufficient animal fats and proteins, and a continual commitment to moral and parental excellence in the parents. This is the mode of parenting in the most advanced places in the West when

parents get tired of politically useless and racially suicidal libertarians setting the standard for excellence in the community.

As the leader in the family, the man must choose what level he will parent at. Most American men content themselves to parenting somewhere between the socializing and helping modes, using elements of both but the helping mode to a much smaller extent. The element of self-reflection comes into play for any forays into the helping or peaceful parenting modes. Modern culture, as influenced by the gatekeepers of the television era and the international corporations of the Internet era, is set against self-reflection. For the few willing to pierce the fog of bigotry, propaganda on "toxic masculinity", white guilt, and intersectionality is floated out to keep seeking types confused and self-defeating. Thankfully, the deluge unleashed by social media ventures before censorship clampdowns in the wake of the 2016 election has ensured that philosophy will reach a broader and broader audience. Reason and evidence that undoes state power has been unleashed into the world.

Self-reflection is critical to achieving the highest modes of parenting because most of the Western populace has been programmed with toxic messaging intended to prevent them from attaining true moral excellence in any shape or form, let alone in parenting. When you are able to understand your own capacity to disrupt higher order parenting processes, whether from trauma experienced in childhood or from propaganda, you begin to take ownership and responsibility for parenting standards that helped to usher in the post-WWII era. You stop being an agent for racial fratricide with punitive notions of controlling others. You take a collaborative approach to your relationships and champion a kind of personal comportment that is increasingly difficult for the state to regulate, much less perceive. Lloyd deMause, funnily enough, would never tell you this because he's a liberal on the constant lookout for Nazi boogeymen.

It is important not to get stuck in the trap of the assumptions of the helping mode of parenting. Such people usually are always libertarians that want to participate in black and grey markets until state power eventually dissipates. These people are smug and conflict avoidant. They have a "wait it out" attitude that does not actively contribute to the battle against evil. They read their non-violent communication books, attend obscure anarchist conferences, compare Donald Trump to their idealistic standards, and are generally weak in their dealings with one another in an effort not to fall out of "helping".

Peaceful parenting is causing a big stir as many prominent conservatives call themselves such or a variation like "gentle parent"[76]. Peaceful parenting, as I argued in my essay *Nihilist Parents Aren't Peaceful Parents*[77], involves the recognition that if state power is ceded to people from child abusive cultures such as the entire Third World, humanity's chance at continual moral improvement will be mortally endangered and probably snuffed out forever. The path to a peaceful society involves both a de-escalation of state power but also the responsibility that the state apparatus not fall into the hands of some banana republic level tyrant, like Alexandra Ocasio Cortez or Bernie Sanders. Should America continue to become Mexico, parenting will devolve and so will general intelligence levels. White men cannot cloister themselves away in the hope that the barbaric cultures of the world will leave them alone. They must draw lines in the stand, make distinctions and categorizations, practice healthy boundaries, and

---

[76] Jenna Jameson Instagram: https://www.instagram.com/jennacantlose/
[77] https://medium.com/@stevenfranssen/nihilist-parents-arent-peaceful-parents-7f070f332721

when left no other option, fight. Otherwise, as in barbaric cultures, the children will be plundered. People stuck in the helping mode lack this sense of self-preservation. They are all too happy to help anyone unconditionally. This results in all manner of racial animosities and a host of welfare programs. At best, they place themselves at the libertarian fringe as mentioned in the previous paragraph. The peaceful parent knows better.

More on parenting in a moment.

Low time preference is the preference for future satisfaction over present satisfaction, or future good over present good. Valuable personal traits that contribute to a low time preference are suppression and forbearance. Suppression is not to be confused with repression. Repression is the rejection from consciousness painful or disagreeable ideas, memories, feelings, or impulses. Suppression is the conscious inhibition of an impulse. Suppression is self-management with an awareness of future goals. Forbearance is similar but operates more on a conceptual level than the mere control of impulses.

A masculine man will work to understand himself better in order to improve the future circumstances of his family, his friends, and his people. You will know a low time preference man by the following markers:

-emphasis on savings

-investment, compounding interest, and asset acquisition mindset

-protection of personal reputation

-fulfillment of contracts, even at a loss

-caretaking of personal effects

-consistent quality of diet and exercise

-cultivation of personal and professional network

-contingencies made for eventual decrease in personal economic productivity

Conversely, a high time preference, effeminate or liberal man will disregard future good for present good. You will know a low time preference man by the following markers:

-emphasis on spending

-loans, debt, consumer credit, and reckless personal spending

-disregard for personal reputation

-nixing of contracts for personal reasons

-neglect of personal effects

-inconsistent, low quality diet and exercise

-narcissistic, dramatic use of personal and professional networks

-avoidance of knowledge of eventual decrease in personal economic productivity

Impulse control is what allows for higher order reasoning and long-term planning. Habitual onanists, drug users, money spenders, and gluttons fail at laying down a long-term path of self-sustained virtue for themselves. The allure of nihilistic release into addiction and depression is simply too much for them. A person can undo any positive benefits they could see from having been born with a higher IQ by choosing a high time preference path.

Despite the best efforts of the legacy media to gaslight the public into believing otherwise, testosterone helps men maintain impulse control[78]. A study out of Massachusetts has shown that total testosterone levels have been dropping by 1.2% every year[79]. A man born in 1970 has 20% less testosterone than his father did at the same age. The cause of this dramatic drop in testosterone is not fully clear but a confluence of factors is surely at play.

One potential cause of America's testosterone loss can be attributed to diet. Animal fats contain cholesterol. Cholesterol is a molecule that has been assailed by experts for the past 40 years. Cholesterol is a key element involved in the synthesis of testosterone and other key hormones. The graph that follows illustrates how the introduction of low-fat guidelines by the US government in the 1970's has correlated with increasing obesity[80].

---

[78] https://www.ncbi.nlm.nih.gov/pmc/articles/PMC4332159/
[79] https://www.thebodywellusa.com/the-hard-truth-for-men-declining-testosterone-levels-worldwide/
[80] https://www.healthy-holistic-living.com/high-cholesterol-alzheimers/?t=dm

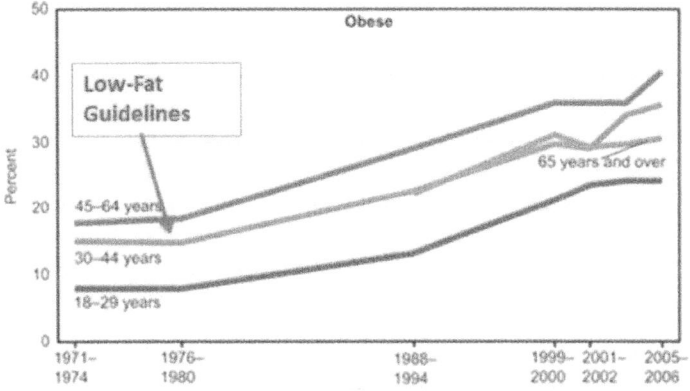

Other culprits for the societal drop in testosterone are:

1. The prevalence of xenoestrogens in massively produced consumer products. Xenoestrogens are a type of xenohormone that imitates estrogen. Men are exposed to this toxic substance on a daily basis.

2. Sedentary lifestyles leading to low libido, low sperm fertility, exhaustion, and depressive disorders.

3. Feminism effeminizes men and removes them from positions of influence, leadership, and power.

Common symptoms of low testosterone in men include[81]:

-low sex drive

-erectile dysfunction

---

[81] https://www.cbsnews.com/pictures/11-warning-signs-of-low-testosterone/4/

-low seminal fluid levels

-fatigue

-decreased energy

-mood problems

-irritability

-reduced muscle mass

-excess body fat

If you are experiencing any of these symptoms and suspect you may be suffering from low testosterone, it is worth consulting with an endocrinologist at a hormone health clinic. Your family practitioner will be bound by a host of Obama era regulations and warnings designed to inhibit over prescription of testosterone treatments. He or she will be less inclined to help you. Also be aware that medically acceptable standards for testosterone levels today are far below what the *average* testosterone levels of men in the 1950's were. Do not accept medical stonewalling intended to keep you effeminized.

Back to parenting.

Successful parenting is a form of investment. "You can always look to how a farm is tended and know the farmer," Robert Newton Peck once wrote[82]. Successful parenting is a process of curiosity, love, empiricism, protection, and education. A masculine man will bear children who grow up to be philosophical, competent, virtuous, joyful, and loving. The masculine man understands that the future good relies on his excellence as a father. There are no government

---

[82] Troy, A., Green, P., & Peck, R. N. (1988). The Day no pigs would die (Robert N. Peck). Palatine, IL: A. Troy, P. Green.

guarantees and entitlements coming down the line, especially once the Boomers have mostly died off. Social Security and Medicare will be totally bankrupt in less than 25 years, regardless of how the Federal government tries to extend its credit. A masculine man knows hard times are coming. He must prepare his children so that when they are adults, they can work in harmony with him to ensure the next generation's survival.

Low time preference also requires a certain bearing be brought on inter-tribal relations. The masculine man deals with outsiders in a firm but fair manner. He greets everyone as a friend the first time he has contact with them and immediately reciprocates whatever respect or lack of respect they give him in response. He holds his center in his dealings with outsiders. Good relations can always be had with outsiders but that depends on the masculinity of the parties involved. Liberalism poisons diplomatic relations by removing masculine males from the decision-making process in favor of the minority de jure. Only masculine leaders can resist the temptations of welfare, warfare, and tyranny. The masculine leaders of today establish a hegemony for the leaders of tomorrow.

One look at the childless leaders of European Union states compared to their Eastern European counterparts will inform you of who truly has skin in the game. The major EU leaders like Angela Merkel, the skinny French guy who was a Rothschild banker, and Swedish Stefan Löfven have driven their countries into demographic disaster. Eastern Europe, on the other hand, is loaded with male leaders who want to keep the fundamental character of their nations. "Hungary's conservative prime minister Viktor Orbán has announced seven family-friendly government programs that will encourage Hungarians to have children as the country rejects the European

Union's progressive mass migration agenda," underscores a Breitbart headline on Hungary's newest social policies[83]. The article reads,

> Two of the most ambitious of the seven programs, however, are directed at women. In one scheme, the government will give a loan of ten million Forints (£27,385/$35,230) to every woman under 40 who marries for the first time. One third of the loan's repayment would be waived upon the birth of the first child, further concessions for the second, with the entire loan being written off after the birth of a third child. The other program would see women who have raised four or more children being exempt from paying income tax for life.
>
> Both of these women-focused policies were revealed the day before the progressive Council of Europe human rights commissioner claimed that Hungary had backslid on women's rights, as well as those of migrants.
>
> With Hungary's 2016 birth rate at 1.45 children per woman — well below the 2.1 needed for natural population maintenance — the Fidesz-Christian Democratic People's Party government hopes these measures will encourage citizens to start and grow families.
>
> "In our minds, immigration means surrender," said Mr. Orbán."

Other nations joining the masculine push to assure a future for its children include Poland, with a "maternal pension" for women who have raised four or more children, and Italy whose deputy prime minister Matteo Salvini has begun mass deportations of migrants. Salvini has said, "a country which does not create children is destined

---

[83] https://www.breitbart.com/europe/2019/02/11/we-need-hungarian-children-orban-tax-breaks-families/

to die." While the liberal media will busy itself maligning these efforts with invocations of Nazi Germany, these nations will busy themselves with setting the course for Western Civilization in the generations to come.

A nation that follows childless leaders is a nation that has surrendered its masculinity. Whether nations such as the U.K., Germany, and Sweden can return masculine leaders back to prominence is yet to be seen. Domestication is deeply entrenched in the heart of the West. The masculine leaders of Poland, Hungary, and Italy are investing in the children of their nations. As prominent black conservative Jesse Lee Peterson has said, "If we lose white folks, we lose America! That's why I always tell white people to have truckloads of white babies. Hungary is doing it right."

Socio-Sexual Hierarchy

Men have never survived the elements, nature, outsiders, or any other mortal threat by remaining "solo practitioners" of masculinity. Men have always banded together for mutual aid, exploration, and conquest. These groups of men are arranged by a hierarchy. Vox Day explains,

> "Alpha: The alpha is the tall, good-looking guy who is the center of both male and female attention. The classic star of the football team who is dating the prettiest cheerleader. The successful business executive with the beautiful, stylish, blonde, size zero wife. All the women are attracted to him, while all the men want to be him, or at least be his friend. At a social gathering like a party, he's usually the loud, charismatic guy telling self-flattering stories to a group of attractive

women who are listening with interest. However, alphas are only interested in women to the extent that they exist for the alpha's gratification, physical and psychological, they are actually more concerned with their overall group status.

Lifetime sexual partners = 4x average+.

Beta: Betas are the good-looking guys who aren't as uniformly attractive or socially dominant as the Alpha, but are nevertheless confident, attractive to women, and do well with them. At the party, they are the loud guy's friends who showed up with the alcohol and who are flirting with the tier one women and cheerfully pairing up with the tier two women. Betas tend to genuinely like women and view them in a somewhat optimistic manner, but they don't have a lot of illusions about them either. Betas tend to be happy, secure in themselves, and are up for anything their alpha wants to do. When they marry, it is not infrequently to a woman who was one of the alpha's former girlfriends.

Lifetime sexual partners = 2-3x average.

Delta: The normal guy. Deltas are the great majority of men. They can't attract the most attractive women, so they usually aim for the second-tier women with very limited success, and stubbornly resist paying attention to all of the third-tier women who are comfortably in their league. This is ironic, because deltas would almost always be happier with their closest female equivalents. When a delta does manage to land a second-tier woman, he is constantly afraid that she will lose interest in him and will, not infrequently, drive her into the very loss of interest he fears by his non-stop dancing of attendance upon her. In a social setting, the deltas are the men clustered together in groups, each of them making an occasional foray towards various small gaggles of women before beating a hasty retreat when direct eye contact and engaged responses are not forthcoming. Deltas tend to put the female sex on pedestals and have overly optimistic expectations of them; if a man rhapsodizes about his better half or is an inveterate White Knight, he is almost certainly a delta. Deltas like women, but find them mysterious, confusing, and are sometimes secretly a little afraid of them.

Lifetime sexual partners = 1-1.5x average

Gamma: The introspective, the unusual, the unattractive, and all too often the bitter. Gammas are often intelligent, usually unsuccessful with women, and not uncommonly all but invisible to them, the gamma alternates between placing women on pedestals and hating the entire sex. This mostly depends upon whether an attractive woman happened to notice his existence or not that day. Too introspective for their own good, gammas are the men who obsess over individual women for extended periods of time and supply the ranks of stalkers, psycho-jealous ex-boyfriends, and the authors of excruciatingly romantic rhyming doggerel. In the unlikely event they are at the party, they are probably in the corner muttering darkly about the behavior of everyone else there... sometimes to themselves. Gammas tend to have a worship/hate relationship with women, the current direction of which is directly tied to their present situation. However, they are sexual rejects, not social rejects.

Lifetime voluntary sexual partners = .5x average

Omega: The truly unfortunate. Omegas are the social losers who were never in the game. Sometimes creepy, sometimes damaged, often clueless, and always undesirable. They're not at the party. It would never have crossed anyone's mind to invite them in the first place. Omegas are either totally indifferent to women or hate them with a borderline homicidal fury.

Sigma: The outsider who doesn't play the social game and managed to win at it anyhow. The sigma is hated by alphas because sigmas are the only men who don't accept or at least acknowledge, however grudgingly, their social dominance. (NB: Alphas absolutely hate to be laughed at and a sigma can often enrage an alpha by doing nothing more than smiling at him.) Everyone else is vaguely confused by them. In a social situation, the sigma is the man who stops in briefly to say hello to a few friends accompanied by a Tier 1 girl that no one has ever seen before. Sigmas like women but tend to be contemptuous of them. They are usually considered to be strange. Gammas often like to think they are sigmas, failing to understand that sigmas are not social rejects, they are at the top of the social hierarchy despite their refusal to play by its rules.

Lifetime sexual partners = 4x average+.

Lambda: Those men who have quite literally no interest in conventional male-female sexual relations. They clearly have their own hierarchy of sorts, but I can't say that I know much about it other than it appears to somehow involve youth, free weights, and mustaches.

Lifetime sexual partners = 10x average+.

Now, it is important to keep in mind that it serves absolutely no purpose to identify yourself in some manner that you think is "better" or higher up the hierarchy. No one cares what you think you are and your opinion about your place in the social hierarchy is probably the opinion that matters least. There is no good or bad here, there is only what happens to be observable in social interaction. Consider: alphas seemingly rule the roost and yet they live in a world of constant conflict and status testing. Sigmas usually acquired their outsider status the hard way; one seldom becomes immune to the social hierarchy by virtue of mass popularity in one's childhood. Betas... okay, betas actually have it pretty good. But the important thing to keep in mind is that you can't improve your chances of success in the social game if you begin by attempting to deceive yourself as to where you stand vis-a-vis everyone else around you.[84]"

The categories of the Socio-Sexual Hierarchy are generally inborn. Personality remains remarkably similar over a lifetime and there is no use in pretending to be something you are not. Knowing the hierarchy *does* allow a man to compensate for his weaknesses and further mobilize his strengths in the service of his tribe. A tribe does not have to contain every one of the categories, but larger political and business organizations generally contain members of each of the categories.

It is exceedingly difficult to create an Alpha. You can take an Alpha and hurt his sense of self-worth until he's a Beta, emotionally terrorize him in childhood until he's a Gamma, or put him in situations he's bound to fail in until he's disengaged and becomes a Sigma. The only type of men who can break into Alpha territory are Betas. They have elements of the Alpha in their personality. Deltas lack the flash and sexual charisma to become Alphas. Gammas are simply too prone to self-absorption. Sigmas can't be Alphas unless they were Alphas early in their development.

Betas run into the most problems when they confuse themselves for Alphas. They fail to recognize their lack of uniform attractiveness or they operate for too long in a vacuum absent any Alphas. A Beta needs an Alpha, in order to be his most effective Self. This doesn't mean he is guaranteed to struggle on his own. He will cap out to the best of his abilities, if he is motivated, and will fail to break through to a certain extent without an Alpha. Alphas can be Beta if they run into an Alpha that has a higher sexual market value and financial capabilities. Betas are more prone to relaxing into a

---

[84] https://alphagameplan.blogspot.com/2011/03/socio-sexual-hierarchy.html

secondary role when they meet an Alpha, regardless of how the Alpha ranks according to other Alphas in the environment.

Deltas run into the most problems when they lack work ethic. They do not have the natural attractiveness of a Beta or an Alpha. They lack the charm that attractiveness brings. Without a good work ethic, Deltas are left more vulnerable to female evil. They are less able to plug themselves into hierarchies that automatically weed out crazy women. Given their tendency to put women on a pedestal, it becomes all too easy for the less hardworking Deltas to be picked off by women who will be hypergamous or exploitive. A Delta lives or dies by his work ethic and he needs Betas and Alphas to ensure he stays close to the brotherhood.

Gammas cause all sorts of problems in general but every now and then one in their ranks will do something spectacular, usually of an intellectual nature, that keeps the Gamma class pertinent to the brotherhood. Gammas cause the most problems when they have paired their bitter tendencies with the irreverent ideology of post-modernism. They step outside the hierarchy by refusing to acknowledge its validity. In their bitterness they will either try to siphon off Deltas and Betas into nihilism or they will gradually turn into Omegas out of social isolation. Alphas do well to thoroughly vet Gammas when they come near, to never fully let their guards down in the presence of a Gamma, and to rally social ostracism against the Gamma when he tries to pull others into his nihilism and into his delusion that he is actually a Sigma. If allowed too close into the brotherhood, a Gamma can set back a hierarchy months or even years when he inevitably "checks out". A Gamma's intelligence must be in the service of the hierarchy, not at its expense.

Omegas need therapy and comprehensive weight lifting regimes. No Alpha or Beta in their right mind will ever recruit an Omega into the brotherhood. The burden of the Omega falls squarely on the shoulders of the Omega and all too often his burden falls onto the state. Omegas are deliberately kept out of the reproductive pool because they are the sickly runts of the litter. However, human choice does allow the Omega - especially in free market conditions - to improve his lot.

Sigmas are Bruce Wayne types. They're much rarer than delusional Gammas try to convince themselves of. The Sigma gains pole position by inborn talent that he hones to a sharp point. His problems arise when he fails to remain relevant. Sentimentality too often derails the Sigma's dominant position. Many Sigmas play the game for a time in their youth and check out as they get older. Unlike the Gamma, who does not have it in him to get to the top, the Sigma can always put in the effort and get to the top so long as he doesn't let his skills and talents rot.

The importance of contributing to a hierarchy cannot be understated, regardless of your position within it. I said as much in the very first essay of my previous book *Rise And Fight*. The modern welfare state has taken so much of the danger out of life. Men are no longer incentivized to band together in order to advance the interests of the tribe. Yet, the welfare state will implode sooner than later, and those who retained their hierarchies will advance in the wake of its death. Aloof men who chose to remain absorbed in the feeding trough of globalism will find themselves removed from the gene pool. Isolation does a man no good. By contributing to a hierarchy, a man enriches the life of a brotherhood and a community. He contributes his labor, his thought, his inspiration, his finances, his attention, and his abilities. The strongest tribes thrive and survive. They dominate and self-promote. They endure attack and subversion from outsiders. This is the natural order and it will come back stronger than ever once central bankers and socialists lose their standing in the world. Better to start now by contributing than waiting until it's too late.

Nigel Farage had this to say of Victor Orbán:

> Orbán actually believes in things. He does not sheepishly, slavishly go along with the European project as he firmly believes in the concept of the nation-state. He clearly is a strong defender of, as he sees, the Hungarian culture and is not afraid to say and do these things despite huge criticism from the European Union.[85]

This is a compliment from a natural Beta working in the role of an Alpha, Nigel Farage, to a natural Alpha who overcame considerable odds to lead his Hungarian tribe back to prominence. Both men are bound by the ideal of nationalism, of contributing to one's own tribe, and hence they enjoy a healthy alliance despite being from different tribes. The natural order favors them. Farage builds up his own tribe by extolling the virtues of another tribe. He practices suppression by refusing to call for the destruction of the enemy within as he knows that his own tribe is still too weak to surmount the malevolent EU and the central bankers.

A hierarchy retains its virtue so long as it is aligned with the natural order. Alphas can be corrupted, usually by women or by Gammas, into steering their tribes off course. A tribe that fails to self-correct, usually through the competition of more righteous Alphas coming to the fore, will lose its virtue and descend into chaos.

---

[85] https://voiceofeurope.com/2019/02/farage-viktor-orban-is-the-future-of-europe/

Members of a hierarchy contribute to a tribe's "immune system" by putting pressure to be virtuous on the Alphas and Betas. Healthy, mature Alphas and Betas don't necessarily need this pressure, but they do take a comfort in its presence. It means their tribe members have skin in the game and can be relied upon when important junctures present themselves, such as conflict with another tribe or a refocusing of values in response to the social and political environments. A tribe whose members content themselves to put their heads down and work is susceptible to subversion from outside influences, such as the Evangelical churches by the internationalist tribe. A tribe retains its virtue when it is committed to its own healthy existence, first and foremost. Therefore, the world powers who have led the globe into disaster are so deeply threatened by the rise of Western tribalism.

The Zoomer Worldview

There is a moral tension expressing itself as contentiousness present in young, white males born circa 1998 or later that has been nowhere near as present in the Millennial or Gen-X generations. While the memes are too numerous for most non-Zoomers to keep track of, I profess, some of the more notable ones to break into public awareness recently have been the T-pose, the Halo theme being sung in bathrooms, and "subscribe to PewDiePie".

The T-pose is achieved when the Zoomer puts his feet together and spreads his arms straight out to resemble a Christian cross, a symbol that signifies Jesus Christ's sacrifice for humankind and Christian respect for his sacrifice. The T-pose is also related to video gaming because it is the pose avatars generally make in character customization screens. The T-pose also has the contentious element in it because young white men will employ the pose in small groups either to humorously corral in a young white girl or to keep non-members at bay. This meme arose at a time when the "Deus Vult" meme was starting to wind down, a saying meant to embolden ethnic Westerners in the face a Third World migration crisis featuring a heavy Islamic presence in Europe - reminiscent of the Moor invasions of the Middle Ages.

The Halo theme being sung in the choral style in public school bathrooms is less exclusive to young white males as many viral videos of performances featuring many non-white young men taking their part. The Halo theme is particularly relevant to the first generation raised wholly after the mass proliferation of console video gaming. Halo for the Xbox console remains a high-water mark in the video gaming canon because the all-male production team crafted a truly excellent gaming experience that pitted young, mostly white, soldiers against outside invading forces. There was not a drop of political correctness in the original Halo nor was there even the pretense of garnering empathy for the alien forces attacking the human species. The Xbox console generation of gaming was the last time video game productions were not infested with political correctness. Large corporations bound by affirmative action laws eventually took over the industry. A cadre of feminist commentators and developers nudged out "the good old boys club" by 2014, as evidenced by the GamerGate controversy. Since Gamergate, no group has been more targeted, vilified, and verbally abused than gamers. The choral unison of the Halo theme brings young men together in a way that popular music and cinema simply has not. The theme is a reminder of the duress outside forces have brought upon young guys who just want to game. They just want to play games that are excellent, free of political correctness, and non-Japanese. It is important to note that the Halo theme is sung in boy's bathrooms, where girls are prohibited from entering.

The "Subscribe to PewDiePie" meme that is everywhere on the Internet as of this writing stems out of the competition between PewDiePie, the most popular YouTuber for several years running, and T-Series, an Indian record label and film production company. Both channels are vying for the distinction of having the most subscriptions on the YouTube platform. Internet usage in India is rapidly climbing[86] with somewhere around 3 people per second logging onto the web for the first time in their lives. Since T-Series is the largest music company in India, with a 35% share of the music market there, and relies on upwards of 20 uploads a day to achieve subscriptions, it is hard to see how PewDiePie - a Swedish YouTuber living in the UK - will maintain his lead. The Internet has largely

---

[86] https://www.statista.com/topics/2157/internet-usage-in-india/

proliferated throughout the West. PewDiePie, whose content is largely built on the meme power of the West, has very few emerging markets to tap into. For PewDiePie to be similarly positioned as T-Series is to India, his longstanding market share in the music industry would need to approach Sony's $71 billion in sales in 2016[87]. Instead, PewDiePie has made $60.5 million from his YouTube channel and endorsements since 2014[88]. With no emerging market and a meager fraction of the T-Series war chest, PewDiePie presses on by sheer memetic power. Zoomers have mobilized to keep him on top. A group of five young Millennials made the news at the most recent Superbowl by wearing "Sub 2 PewDiePie" on their shirts while sitting in the endzone. They were seen on the live broadcast at several points.

The symbolism of the "Subscribe to PewDiePie" meme is particularly cogent when you consider PewDiePie, a heterosexual gamer Swede who hints at having conservative politics now and then, is pitted against a Third World conglomerate of Indians who have rigged the YouTube system in their favor. This is a clash of cultures occurring with a demographic crisis of Third World invasion lingering in the background. PewDiePie is a hero to anyone opposed to the socialist, child rape culture of India. As an entertainer working on meme power, he reflects back to Zoomers and younger Millennials the more joyous and wonderful aspects of their besieged culture. He has stood toe to toe with some of the most evil corporations in the United States, including The Wall Street Journal[89] and Disney, and come out victorious. He has lambasted the YouTube Corporation for attempting to rewrite viral history as a sterilized, LGBTQ prominent,

---

[87] https://www.sony.net/SonyInfo/News/Press/201610/16-1003E/index.html
[88] https://www.celebritynetworth.com/richest-celebrities/actors/pewdiepie-net-worth/
[89] https://www.wsj.com/articles/disney-severs-ties-with-youtube-star-pewdiepie-after-anti-semitic-posts-1487034533

monstrosity where has-beens like Will Smith are supposed to lead the youth into a brighter tomorrow[90]. PewDiePie recently followed such philosophical luminaries as Lauren Southern, Sam Hyde, and Stefan Molyneux on Twitter. He is a massive wrench in the global political elite's plan to flood the First World with the Third and wipe out any ethnic consciousness on the part of white males. He, along with a few choice others such as Alex Jones, holds the center of the resistance in the information war for the soul of the West. PewDiePie is beloved by Zoomers and reflects back to them, in small doses, the racial awareness[91] that infuriates the mainstream media and their litigious lackeys, the SPLC and ACLU.

Michael C. Reichert, Ph.D., author of *How To Raise A Boy*, writes:

> A new study by a team of researchers with my Center for the Study of Boys' and Girls' Lives at the University of Pennsylvania found something that stood out in qualitative commentary offered by male teens. In response to schools' sincere commitments to diversity and equality, growing notes of despair, anger, and resentment have arisen from boys who complain of being "judged," "attacked," "ignored," and "silenced." These young males say they are now "afraid to be who they are," and believe "their opinions do not matter." As one explained, "I am a white, conservative, heterosexual male, and I'm proud of who I am. I feel that I can't share my

---

[90] "YouTube Rewind 2018 but it's actually good" https://www.youtube.com/watch?v=By_Cn5ixYLg
[91] https://heavy.com/entertainment/2017/02/pewdiepie-disney-anti-semitic-videos-maker-studios-felix-kjellberg-funny-guys/

opinions without being ridiculed and accused of microaggressions.[92]

The schools these Pennsylvania Zoomers go to are, "sincerely committed to diversity and equality". Diversity simply means "less white people". There is no push to make non-White countries more "diverse". Equality is simply cultural Communism, where the intelligence differences between the races are completely denied and anyone who exceeds beyond the lowest common denominator must be bludgeoned into compliance by state power. White men built the West. Young white men who are alive today were supposed to be the inheritors of this spectacular and unique success. It is a question of inherited intelligence and inherited personality traits. The others, en masse, did not create the West and are fundamentally incapable - in aggregate - to "drive the machinery of freedom" of the West. The East Asians, who have a higher average IQ than whites, have created their own Eastern society of skyscrapers and economic productivity often based on currency manipulation and free trade swindles. The Jews, who have a higher average IQ than whites, have created their own Semitic society backed by American military might, technological innovation, and Talmudic cultural principles. Only Western people create the West. Some non-Westerners can more or less assimilate in their lifetimes, but the large majority and a large majority of their children vote for more socialism[93].

The institutions these boys attend are committed, by law, to their ethnic and cultural displacement. As a result, the boys complain

---

[92] https://www.psychologytoday.com/us/blog/the-power-connection/201901/look-considering-the-boy-behind-the-mask
[93] "Second-Generation Americans: A Portrait of the Adult Children of Immigrants"
http://www.pewsocialtrends.org/2013/02/07/second-generation-americans/

of being judged, attacked, ignored, and silenced. Their teachers, who vote largely Democrat[94], are culprits in the verbal abuse slathered on these boys. But so are their fellow, non-white students. As Twitter user with the handle Calvizzles tweeted out, "A white man raising their hand to comment in a history class is violence". This racial vitriol received over 2,100 retweets and 10,900 likes in the span of five days[95]. The user's follow-up comment to his original vitriol was, "Before you try to argue with me, PLEASE consider: I don't care." What else is this young black male trying to communicate but, "your opinions don't matter" to anyone speaking up for white males? The user has not been removed from Twitter for racial hatred as Twitter upholds a policy where conservatives are constantly deplatformed while the rest of the world is entitled to hurl abuse at them[96].

These kinds of anti-white verbal attacks are commonplace in the public schools and on social media. The Democrat teachers allow this to happen. After all, the Democrat party, at a policy level, is the party committed to the taxation and displacement of whites for the benefit of the Third World. Conservative, heterosexual males are not allowed to share their opinions without being ridiculed and accused of microaggressions. The postmodernist, cultural Marxist opinionmakers in the media, Department of Education, tech giants, lobbying groups, and Hollywood are ideologically committed to shutting down and ridiculing these young men before they have a chance to vote for smaller government and immigration restriction as

---

[94] https://www.edweek.org/ew/articles/2017/12/13/survey-paints-political-portrait-of-americas-k-12.html
[95] https://twitter.com/OrwellNGoode/status/1092485849693020166
[96] "TECHTwitter Bans Popular Conservative Account On Christmas Eve For Criticism of Pedophilia"
https://bigleaguepolitics.com/twitter-bans-popular-conservative-account-on-christmas-eve-for-criticism-of-pedophilia/

adults. Such a course would reduce the political mayhem these groups have unleashed on the American middle class.

Since the most vigorous tend to be the young and since heterosexual white conservative males tend to make the best arguments for freedom and social order, they must be shouted down. Anyone who watched the run up to the 2016 election saw example after example of young Trump supporters being shouted down in college campuses, before Trump rallies, in public spaces, and anywhere else that liberals could get at them. Any assemblage of more than one person in a MAGA hat was cause for media hysteria, a harkening to the Nazis and the Holocaust, and Third World panic of the second coming of colonialism. The term "Trump Derangement Syndrome" came to prominence when countless mental health counselors in liberal strongholds had client after client come to them with distress they attributed to Donald J. Trump. The anti-white hysteria, brought on by big government mass migration policies and welfare distribution, runs ever deeper in a "browning of America"[97]. The most vigorous of any political movement must be stopped. The trend toward racial consciousness, allowed for every group outside of whites, is spearheaded by unapologetic, young white males. Every effort must be made to shout them down, confuse them in a panic, turn them into homosexuals, or outright physically assault them in public spaces.

The Zoomer worldview acknowledges the battering ram of non-white envy, the treachery of hyper sexualization of young white females, the war against gamers, and the institutional array besieging the prospect of another white male political hegemony and

---

[97] https://twitter.com/benshapiro/status/875730927002963968

meritocracy in the West. The Zoomer worldview does include young black, Asian, and Hispanic conservatives but it is fundamentally the ingroup strategy of white, heterosexual males. These trespasses are shouldered by the Zoomer with the grace of SpongeBob SquarePants, whose cartoon heyday peaked during the early childhoods of Zoomers. SpongeBob, in many respects, is a Christ-like figure. He is persistent in making the world a better place, maintaining his sobriety and chastity, and he bears the brutality of those around him as long as possible until he finally responds with incredible fury, energy, and resolution.

Zoomers will rise up. It is an inevitability. Whether the rest of the political world is willing to lay down their bloodied daggers remains to be seen.

Making Friends & Building Community

The global elite want the average white American atomized and isolated. The less unity Americans possess, the easier they are to scatter to the winds. The strength of the family is the weakness of the state. Instead of family values, we are given a steady drip of every conceivable drama that will pull people out of their home lives. The media promotes race war, class divisions, gender confusion and discord, and hatred for anyone who is an effective reformer in these categories. The answer to these problems is more freedom, not socialism and sectarian violence. The leftists may have a special animosity toward heterosexual whites, but they are all too happy to use minorities as mascots to achieve their political ends. Globalism is forced wealth redistribution from all working classes, regardless of race, into the hands of the elite.

Building community is one of the non-political answers to the impending death of the West. I have met many people in the culture war because of my social media contributions, some of whom were guest contributors in my last book *Rise And Fight: Defeat Globalism, Save The West*. Anyone can make meaningful, personal connections with others who share your value over social media. Isn't that the whole point of it? However, an article from *Study Finds* shows that social media isn't the end all be all:

> Brian A. Primack, M.D., Ph.D., director of Pitt's Center for Research on Media, Technology and Health, and his team examined questionnaires in 2014 from 1,787 Americans between the ages of 19 and 32. The surveys sought to see how

often the participants logged onto the 11 most popular social networks and how much time a typical session would last.

The top social media platforms at the time were Facebook, YouTube, Twitter, Google Plus, Instagram, Snapchat, Reddit, Tumblr, Pinterest, Vine and LinkedIn.

The data was then plugged into the Patient-Reported Outcomes Measurement Information System (PROMIS), a tool that evaluates social and mental health in people of all ages, to measure the participants' perceived social isolation.

Those who spent more than two hours a day on social media were twice as likely to show signs of social isolation than participants who spent no more than 30 minutes on the sites. Similarly, young adults who visited the sites at least 58 times in a week were triple the odds of feeling socially isolated than those who only logged onto social media nine times in a week. This held true even when demographic and other control factors were taken into consideration.

Primack and his team considered that social media use could potentially consume a person so much that there's little time for them to enjoy personal, real-world socializing. But the amount of time spent seeing the lives of others could also spark feelings of exclusion or jealousy. Perhaps a user might see a celebration he or she wasn't invited to; or simply viewing a person's photos of a family vacation or other personal event could cause someone to believe their friend enjoys a happier, more fulfilled life than them.

> Building community will take on a personal aspect for anyone with any sense as America culturally and legally fractures.[98]

Social media connections are valuable but their nature changes when one approaches with the idea that social media is a vetting process for in person contact. Online dating is a vehicle for in-person dates. Why can't social media be a vehicle for hanging out and collaborating in person? Social media is a mild crutch for loneliness and loneliness is a killer:

> Loneliness has been found to increase the chance of mortality by 26 percent, as well as increasing the risk of high blood pressure and obesity. In fact, it has now been shown that the impact a lack of social connections has on your health is equivalent to smoking 15 cigarettes a day. Only a few months ago, doctors were warning that loneliness can be as bad for a person's health as living with a long-term serious illness such as diabetes. As a result, it means that patients who are isolated are more likely to visit the doctor, in part just to have human contact, and more likely to be placed on medication as a consequence.[99]

Problems born out of social isolation are not resolved by more social isolation. People who are lonely need to get off their devices and spend time with others.

The nature of a dissident life can be lonely. The major institutions are rife with globalists who have less children, eat their

---

[98] https://www.studyfinds.org/social-media-isolation-study/
[99] https://www.iflscience.com/health-and-medicine/loneliness-is-as-bad-for-your-health-as-smoking-15-cigarettes-a-day/

soy meals, and deliberately ostracize most conservatives they meet as "racists". However, time is not on the side of these people:

> Take a randomly selected sample of 100 liberal adults and 100 conservative adults. According to an analysis of the 2004 General Social Survey -- a bible of data for social scientists -- the liberals would have had 147 kids, while the conservatives would have had 208. That's a fertility gap of 41 percent. Even adjusting for other variables like age and income, there is a gap of 19 percent.[100]

The future for America may be brown but the white future is most certainly conservative. Better these conservatives and their children find social cohesion before America stumbles off its demographic cliff. With endless distractions like video games, social media addiction, movies, shopping, and the tendency of people to shut themselves away in their homes out of social anxiety from living in a multicultural society, it is not so easy to build community. The Internet can and does help!

Practically everyone I know in my personal life I met through my YouTube channel, website, or Twitter profile. I have known plenty of people through the gym and pickup basketball, plenty of people I spent time with in college and high school, co-workers, and musicians from bands I have played in but exceedingly few of these people ever shared my values. None of them ever matched my enthusiasm for philosophy. The Internet allowed me to specialize. I have sought out people who share my highest values and found them.

With YouTube, I have spent the better part of six years uploading presentations, commentaries, interviews, and music that has either been philosophical or has represented some point of view

---

[100] https://www.sfgate.com/opinion/article/Republicans-fertile-future-Through-the-past-2488626.php

or preference of mine. I have been highly selective. I have actively cultivated a comments section of people who add value. I have ~3500 subscribers and most of my interactions with these people have been positive, if not inspiring. As the needs of my family change over time, I will be happy to fiddle with my format so that more people subscribe and so that interest stays fresh.

My website and Twitter work similarly in that they are a deeper dive into my thoughts on what is happening in the world. Anyone non-toxic is free to write me an email, linked on my website, or write me a direct message on Twitter. Often, I am picking up clients to consult but other times I'll be in touch with fellow culture warriors or just honest people who like the way I live. These contacts have been indelible part of my life since I took a public facing role in 2013. I am always looking for new contacts, always open to new friends, and constantly engaged in adding value to the lives of others. The more competent I am at this, the better suited to my values and goals people seem to become - though that isn't always the focus. People are downright interesting, in and of themselves. I find myself reaching out to others who aren't involved in politics or political commentary at least a few times a year.

Talking to people is a subtle art that takes plenty of practice and benefits from a wide variety of contacts. It's not always immediately clear what there is to talk about, especially for people who are more introverted. The best place to start with anyone is to see if there is anything about the other person that provokes curiosity or inspiration for you. Not every relationship has to begin this way. I have made friends through conflict at times. But curiosity is a social glue that binds people together. A fellow may run an antique boutique and your grandmother had a penchant for furniture when you were a kid. A person at the gym may be doing some variation on an exercise you haven't seen before. A person may have a tremendous memory and have plenty of interesting stories to tell. When you reach out with curiosity that is sincere, not out of concern or annoyance, the other person does not have to manage you with defensiveness, evasion, or silence. The other person is free to respond, if they're interested, and engage on something of mutual interest.

Some people are talkers and some people are listeners. Two listeners may not pair well together. Two talkers tend to do alright. A talker and a listener have varying success together, depending on their interests and values.

When building a community, a lot of thought needs to go into a person's function or dysfunction, their ability to contribute in a group setting, their economic capacity, and their commitment to shared values. Your community will go nowhere if you choose a pushover, a pretender, or a lot of the time, a fame chaser. I will highlight each of these personality types later in this book.

You will benefit the most from engaging morally excellent people who understand the stakes the West faces. Moral excellence allows people to contribute to a hierarchy. Self-knowledge helps these morally excellent people not to confuse their roles in the hierarchy, such as a Gamma thinking he's an Alpha. Christianity often helps people to be morally excellent, as the teachings of the New Testament offer tremendous value on living an upright, wholesome life.

You don't have to be the Community Builder. You can join a community that already exists. There aren't very many in existence that are committed to lasting through the demographic and political displacement of whites in the West in a way that is sustainable and morally excellent, but as more and more people *get real* there will be more of these communities. Owen Benjamin is busy cultivating his network of "unBearables". Stefan Molyneux regularly connects people through philosophy. Vox Day has his network of "Reprehensibles". Nick Fuentes has his "Nickers". Ann Coulter and Peter Brimelow have VDare and their immigration patriots. More and more people will enter the fray and find their tribes. Whites may become a diaspora but groups like these inspire a lot of hope.

I have already discussed the question of where to go extensively in the early part of the book. The added dimension here is that you make community a consideration when eyeing strategic relocation in the face of American balkanization. This will probably be an easy question for you if you have plenty of good people around in person. I know a homeschooling family in the Midwest who has a marvelous community around them. These people will do well for the next 15-25 years. Not everyone is so fortunate.

Quality people matter the most, despite what GDP junkies at conservative thinktanks would have you believe. A lifelong friend is probably worth a couple million dollars in saved health expenses, disaster liability, counseling fees, and general life happiness. Good people make a net contribution to our lives in ways that are often intangible. Living near these people strengthens the bonds, allow for contingencies to life's challenges, and provides an opportunity to raise children alongside other adults with shared values. Atomization means no mutual support. No mutual support as America becomes Mexico means there are less adults around to man the fort when the liberal mobs take to the streets and drag people out of their homes.

I would choose proximity to good people over most legal considerations on the books, such as rates of taxation or even the general demographics in an area. Homeschooling is a bit of a sticking point for me and there are a few states that are far too invasive in the lives of homeschooled children for my preference[101] of peace and harmony in the home. With enough good people around, most of the challenges of living in a socialized America can be ameliorated, at least for a while.

Networks of mutual support stand the best chance at weathering America's decline. As Democrats take more and more power, there will be no legal guarantees that whites can stave off their own destruction. Mutual support networks are the modus operandi of South Africa, as evidenced by Lauren Southern's documentary *Farmlands*, and they will be how whites in the West survive. Asset acquisition, contingency strategies, rapport, childrearing, and an empirical commitment to the changing conditions of the decline will be the points of emphasis in a community that seeks to last.

Now for some discussion on "enemies within" that can wreck a community if left unchecked.

---

[101] https://projects.propublica.org/graphics/homeschool

Enemies Within

Men Who Settle (an entry from stevenfranssen.com)

> "The way you time travel as a man is when you're 22, you're 17, when you're 24 you just fuck around a lot and before you know it you'll be 30, you'll be 40, you'll have fucking nothing. 'Bye, four years! I thought I would have learned more by now. I got a tattoo and worked in a store. I thought I would be somewhere better by now.' Shack up with your high school or college girlfriend. 22-year-old guys know a lot about relationships so it's important to commit and get a girlfriend at age 22."
>
> -Sam Hyde

Men with mommy issues are all too eager to consign their lives away at a far younger age than they are ready for. Coupling up to "save on bills" and feel less guilty about the lack of love in a relationship comes at a terrible price: male achievement.

The cruel fact about Boomer/Gen X era parenting is that most young men (18 to 30) don't have the personal stamina to support a romantic relationship and any degree of career ambition at the same time. For those with attachment issues, the easiest choice is to go into the realm of "feels" with a woman. The current cultural pressure is to serve the needs of women at great personal expense. Men are funneled into coupling up and out of the realm of male achievement. Young men are avoidant of achievement. They have been trained to be so because of massive daycare rates in the 1990's and 2000's and because of the predominance of feminism in the culture and public schooling.

From my personal and professional experience, most men who get into long term relationships at a young age do so because they are isolated from any meaningful connection with other men and because they lack the courage to define themselves in the arena of male achievement. Only a rare few, those who were parented the best or have higher intelligence, can support a long-term relationship and male achievement at the same time. These people are the breadwinners of our society and the backbone of civilization.

I would caution men out there not to use a relationship with a woman as an emotional crutch. Women are far more empowered in today's day and age. It's a bad, emasculating look for a man to rely on that fact by coupling up. Better to spend those four years that Sam Hyde refers to as a single man who is striving to establish himself in a valuable vocation.

If male achievement is at all an opportunity cost for you or has been in getting into a relationship with a woman, you're probably a loser to some degree. There is a price to pay for this kind of arrogance and personal neglect. Toe the line, pay the price, and get moving.

If you haven't compromised yourself in this manner, I applaud you. Our world needs more men like you. Settle the money question before you settle the woman question. Your children will thank you.

The Pushover (from stevenfranssen.com)

The Pushover is a person who is easy to defeat. He walks through life as a victim incapable of putting up resistance.

Some basic examples of the behavior of the pushover:

-cannot assert himself and his preferences to others

-people pleases to people's faces but reverts to his addictions and self-justifications when alone again

-cannot ask for help, nor is he willing to

-makes attempts to "finally be a man" that fail over and over

-listens to sales pitches for long periods of time because he can't say "no"

-relies on women to play the masculine roles in his life (pay his bills, fight his battles, set limits with his children, engage in politics)

-if a woman, accepts and idealizes weakness from the men in her life

-is lampooned by children, treated with annoyance and impatience by them

-holds open doors for people who don't respect him

-acts tough around feminine women but melts like chicken shit when a masculine man comes around

-complains loudly and often about psychosomatic ailments

-lets other dominate his time

-adopts humanitarian causes involving children who cannot assert themselves to him

A pushover can be male or female, but I will focus on the male version. Let's dig into the psychology of who this person is.

The Pushover is formed in childhood by parents who either domineered or neglected him. Domineering parents broke the spirit of the child. Neglectful parents sapped the spirit out of the child. The pushover is sometimes the example of an Alpha or Beta who was made into a Gamma.

The Pushover doesn't take responsibility for his defeats. If he did, he would have to change. He needs to stay within the comforts of mediocrity, conformity, and misery. By being easy to defeat, the pushover remains a nobody, self-sacrificing for the aims of those who either domineer or neglect him as an adult.

The Pushover lives in a personal myth of patheticness that only gains credibility as the defeats and disappointments pile up. The Pushover is surrounded and assailed by hostiles, nitpickers, and verbal abusers out of his own choice. Sometimes he is so defeated that he will self-flagellate to turn away the hostiles. Better to whip oneself with chains than allow others to do it, he thinks. He is his parental abusers incarnate.

Weakness is the calling card of the pushover. His body is stricken with sickly energy. He secretly favors the weak in any conflict. He unconsciously seeks out art that reflects back to him the gnawing emptiness he felt when his parents didn't love him. He will choose art from weak artists with weak messages and lie to himself, telling himself it's actually "strong". He plays "cute" on social media or to anyone he associates with, in the hopes they will give him morsels of sympathy.

If he is malevolent, he justifies his weak personality to the world, hoping to infect others with his madness. He will idealize his preferences and feel relief as the vitality in others around him is drained. The Pushover is not to be idealized. He cannot be counted on in battle. He cannot be pair bonded with because he cannot provide strong guidance or encouragement to anyone. He will not wage the battle against evil. At most he will take up a centrist position and choose to speak up only when it is safe to do so, as cowards do.

Without self-led intervention, the pushover will resign himself completely to a life of misery. This generally happens in a person's mid to late 20's. It's the quarter life crisis of neural plasticity. The choice is: break from the past and form and reform the personality anew or give in to the seeping coldness of nihilism and harden. The worse-off the pushover is, the swifter he will deliver himself to the guillotine. Perhaps he marries the wrong person and even worse, has children with this person, resigning himself to decades of self-sacrifice. Maybe he gives in to Internet pornography and severs his capacity for romance. Or he loses himself in a career path that poisons his spirit or a lesser career that keeps him confined. Some pushovers commit criminal acts upon the innocent to bring on long prison sentences marked by not having to care about one's own needs anymore. The most desperate of the pushovers will kill himself. The years of rage at his awful parents burst out of his emotional armor one last time.

You cannot save or rehabilitate a pushover with your care and love. He does not know how to receive these values. You cannot turn back the clock on his years of self-flagellation with a few vulnerable conversations. His years have accrued to him. They are embedded deep within the bedrock of his personality. A pushover may give you a few meager morsels of affection or attention now and then. It's to keep you around and to pull someone down into the destruction, whether his childhood pattern is to domineer or neglect others. No lie borne out of his self-absorption will ever give you what you need, whether as a friend or for the women – as a lover. Don't let his personal myths overwhelm you, however alluring or charming they may seem. His myths will consume you over time.

Only the pushover can rehabilitate himself. True, dynamic change can only come to him out of the choice to be single and celibate until his personality is fundamentally altered through conscious self-reflection. Anything less is a half measure to be rationalized away by a false conscientious pragmatism that will rob him of fundamental change. He must renounce masturbation and the distraction of the romance rescue fantasy. He must renounce whatever emotional armor he wore during his years of self-harm: nerdiness, cynicism, video gaming, technological enslavement, niche cultures, boredom, isolation, apathy, nihilism, mood altering drugs, or whatever else kept his true feelings at bay.

Redemption can be found for the pushover but only through his own search. The cleansing fire of grieving in solitude and singlehood will burn away his emotional armor and rewrite his psyche. He cannot do this within the context of a romantic relationship because his choice and conduct in changing himself must be entirely self-originated. By choosing this form of independence, he ensures he will not perpetuate his dependency on his future children unconsciously during their development or allow the few slivers of weakness he'd spare to come back into his conscious life in old age when the consequences of his half measures have already accrued.

The job must be done completely, or he cannot attain or offer true love in his lifetime.

Don't try to save the Pushover!

The Pretender

Let's root out the rats and the grifters.

Any person or group of people making a deliberate, consistent, and honest effort at virtue will need to be aware of some of the camouflaging techniques used by those who pretend to be good. People who pretend to be good always have an ulterior motive. This ulterior motive is always to exploit the virtuous party, whether from within or without. These pretenders are morally and psychologically corrupt in that they will never do the difficult personal work it takes to right their wrongs and choose a better path, despite the best efforts of others.

What follows is a rundown of the values most commonly sought for exploitation by a pretender.

1. Moral Sanction

Some pretenders are highly conscientious simply as an inborn trait. Conscientiousness does not automatically mean "disposed to being good". Conscientiousness is an attention to the experiences of others and a knack for detail. This trait is utilized by a pretender to gain the trust of the group by saying the right things at the right times. Virtuous people are often vulnerable to people-pleasing because they can misinterpret shows of kindness as a desire on the part of the pretender to integrate.

Conscientious pretenders need moral sanction, some kind of approval from the virtuous, in order to normalize their intense feelings of guilt and toxic shame. If they can penetrate into the life of someone who is genuinely good, extract approval through people-pleasing and conscientiousness, and use the emotional resource to "kick the can down the road" on their own suffering - they effectively don't have to change at an existential level. Some pretenders, because of their inborn conscientiousness, know at a deep level how messed up and unhealthy they are but they lack the courage to face the pain of completely reorienting their personalities through existential suffering.

Thus, a pretender operates as a social leech upon the virtuous. So long as the sanction of "you're an acceptable person to be around" flows to them, they are satisfied to blend in and not make any waves. The pretender professes knowledge of virtue without actually practicing it. Of course, the more virtuous the target the less the pretender can blend in. But larger groups still provide cover.

2. Financial Support or Excess

Intelligence is a luck of the draw sort of the thing. Many pretenders are born with lower intelligence, it can't be helped. Clear thinking can be helped, and clear thinking often leads to business success. But pretenders are not interested in doing difficult work. They are work averse and if they were born with a lower intelligence, they are incapable of compensating for their work aversion. They simply cannot maintain the effort.

Some of these pretenders will try to find virtuous people to exploit of their monetary resources. This can be anything from a borrowed lunch, a borrowed couch or reduced rent, all the way up to some kind of nepotistic angle on a position they are not suited for. The pretender will beg, borrow, or steal once he is in the good graces of a virtuous person, group, or organization. Since he knows he cannot attain finances on his own, he must pursue other means.

Female pretenders are more successful than males in this regard, especially if they are pretty. A young pretty girl has life on "Easy Mode". She can extract resources at the drop of a hat from nearly any insecure male in the vicinity. When she is a pretender and not just a whore, she brings the added dimension of extracting resources *and* convincing her poor schmucks that they are doing a good thing by enabling her. They will make excuses for her once she's manipulated them. These schmucks will circle the wagons around her if a virtuous person figures out her charade. These are the worst kinds of women and much Western lore is dedicated to stories of their evil.

3. Fulfillment of Unmet Childhood Needs

Some pretenders have been exposed to enough philosophy and psychology that they possess an awareness of the depraved nature of their childhoods. They were not raised well. Does this mean they're willing to do the hard work to recover? Of course not! What they set their sights on is to *manage* their symptoms by managing other people. "You are my 'eat ice cream when I'm lonely' friend'" and "you are the stern father who will set me back on track" are the kinds of attitudes toward others the pretender lives with. Genuine human connection and vulnerability is impossible for the pretender. After all, they live in a fundamentally self-deceptive way.

Loneliness is the biggest need the pretender tries to fill by manipulating others, but it is not the only one. Many pretenders need others to fulfill the childhood roles of their family constellation. A pretender may need not only base mood management but to go into whole perverse narratives with another person. Perhaps there was a chronic bulimic sister in the pretender's history. The pretender will go through all the psychotic steps it takes to induce an eating disorder in another person. Perhaps the pretender's father was absent. The pretender will disrupt a virtuous male's attempts at making himself more available to others by projecting onto the male unwanted feelings of abandonment and disappointment. "This male is always disappointed in me!" the pretender will think to himself.

Pretenders love to play games. They do not want to get real. Not good for anyone looking to contribute to a hierarchy that will endure America's decline.

4. Prestige or Visibility

This is similar to the moral sanction aspect. The more highly conscientious pretenders will feel a need to be *perceived* as a virtuous person, because of the social advantages this position provides, and will posture until they achieve prominence. Once a pretender has established in the minds of others a form of virtue prestige, he or she will work to undermine the position of others in the virtuous hierarchy. No others can be allowed as much prominence or visibility. The pretender is fundamentally an exploiter and will let their envy guide them once they have power. The pretender will use the genuine attention to standards of the truly virtuous people around them, against them. The pretender will try to catch others in their own rules while not applying the rules to themselves. This saps the clout from others. Meanwhile, the pretender directs all eyes away from his own personal life so as to not come under the same scrutiny he so readily applies to others. He will not maintain social media accounts. He will operate in the darkness so long as he has a target to drain.

5. Triangulation of a Third Party

Since the pretender is gifted at ruining the lives of others in a covert manner, she is often willing to lend her skills for evil in the service of doing away with an enemy to the genuinely virtuous. If the virtuous are blinded to the wicked nature of her fighting abilities, they will likely assume benevolence on her part. She fought in an honorable fashion, it is assumed. After all, she fought evil! This is categorically good! But outside of life and death scenarios, it is not always so. And regardless, the virtuous will put pressure on themselves to maintain relations with a pretender who fought in bad faith because evil was vanquished and what is it to an adult to put up some simple boundaries with a bad faith fighter?

This sometimes-necessary measure on the part of the virtuous falls flat when there are children in the equation. Children become exposed to the bad faith fighting style of the pretender and assume its dimensions. After all, the style has some measure of tacit approval in the virtuous community! The virtuous must be careful to inculcate their children with a sense of what is good before exposing them to some of the darker arts of setting pretender sociopaths against even worse sociopaths. In our personal lives, there is no need to "set bad guys against worse guys". There's simply family and religious worship.

Another element of triangulation a pretender can bring into the lives of the virtuous is to stir up resentment against a third party. When arguments fail the pretender, who is generally too lazy to make good arguments, resentment must be stirred up. This can happen against a third party or one of the stragglers in the ranks of the virtuous. The pretender lords over unnecessary conflicts she has stirred up. She basks in her position of the aggrieved while delighting as those around her take her side against the outsider. As the 12th rule of Saul Alinsky's Rules for Radicals states, "Pick the target, freeze it, personalize it, and polarize it." If she can isolate the target from sympathy, through verbal manipulation, she has won.

Sympathy is due to virtuous people. Evil people do not deserve sympathy. When the pretender is exposed for having sowed division, she will cry foul and demand sympathy be given to her. Any measure of sympathy in her direction only enables her to continue to hurt others using the power of the virtuous.

6. Justification of Worldview When Ejected from the Virtuous

A pretender is fundamentally a weak person. He has not practiced virtue, only attained a *knowledge* of it in order to manipulate others. Eventually the pretender is exposed for who he is, usually by the top person in the virtue hierarchy. As the pretender is weak, he does not accept his subsequent ejection from the group with grace. Instead he smolders in resentment not for his genuine guilt but for the fact that he was caught! In this resentment he will flail about and try to drag down as many others in the group as possible in order to "stick it" to his tormentor, the person who had the best sense about him.

It is crucial for the leader in the virtue hierarchy to communicate the manipulation and perversion he perceives in the pretender. Sometimes this is done wholly openly with the pretender in attendance. This is an "intervention" and any healthy, reasonably virtuous person accepts such an act as opportunity to prove themselves worthy. To the pretender, this open discussion was in fact a "sneak attack" and all the more reason to continue to flail and threaten the integrity of the virtuous.

When the pretender is firmly ejected, he will target people with lower standards and self-justify until those people are sufficiently manipulated to give him the sympathy he was unable to extract from the virtuous. Oftentimes the pretender's new targets are a rival group but sometimes they are cobbled together from the pretender's workplace and family life. Who better to extract sympathy for supposed aggrievement than from the people who least challenge the pretender with moral excellence? A pretender is utterly incapable of transitioning to a *more* virtuous group than the one he was ejected from because he cannot fake the credibility of the person or people he wronged. Shit always runs downhill.

The agony of sincerely confronting his toxic nature is too much for the pretender. Instead he will calcify his failure as a moral agent, in the company of mediocre people who will accept little or nothing from him. He will seek out the "loving embrace" of unconditional love - standardless anti-expectation. The pretender often turns to a church or relief organization when he has exhausted the goodwill of anyone formerly willing to relate to him.

7. Fulfillment of Need for Sadism

Since deep down the pretender identifies as someone who is not virtuous, the pretender is fundamentally at odds with a genuinely virtuous person. In his worldview and according to his nervous system's perverse arrangement, he takes secret pleasure in the failings of good people. This is sadism. The bigger the failure, the bigger the dopamine rush for the pretender. Many pretenders, especially those with inborn conscientiousness, will focus on smaller, opportune moments to contribute to the failure of the virtuous. After all, overexposure with an outsized failing may lead to others catching on to his game.

Some pretenders, with little inborn conscientiousness, will "go for the gold". This is especially true of physically attractive pretenders. They possess the universal currency of their arousing looks and can thus afford many more social blowups than those less endowed. The average person is more willing to freeze his own judgement on a person's reputation when the person in question, the pretender, is physically attractive. Pleasure in the failure of the virtuous is at the heart of a pretender.

8. Sex

A pretender abhors standards and works to undermine them at every turn. A person with standards around sex is an unbearable experience for a pretender because of the vulnerable nature of sex's energy exchange between the parties. Much is revealed to an empathetic person about another person through the sex act. Therefore, it is in the pretender's best interests to choose sex partners who are lower in their empathy skills. Why expose him or herself to the discerning eye of a good person in intimate moments? Better to find a virtuous target whose skill threshold with empathy is lower than the pretender's capacity to manipulate. Then, the sex act becomes a source of manipulative power for the pretender.

Women are most often guilty of this sexual manipulation. Some men screw their way into strong sisterhoods, but these are generally male feminists - a very small portion of the adult population. It is the female pretender who screws her way into strong brotherhoods. Of course, a strong brotherhood has standards to keep such women out, but it is folly to underestimate the seductive power of a woman well versed in pretending to be healthy. She has had a lifetime of preying upon others.

It is supremely important to have thorough vetting measures for the people that come into our lives. One crazy person can set us, our families, our friends, and our organizations back months, years, or even permanently. Authenticity and sincere commitment to virtue are precious resources in the world. Better not to assume the presence of these qualities in the personalities of others simply because they are drawn to your message and commitment to virtue. Some pretenders associate and pretend good faith for years before they strike. Nor can we become paranoid and close ourselves off to failure and friction. There is a golden mean that only experience and continual commitment to moral excellence can provide.

Fame Chasers

I see a lot of dysfunction in the political dissident movement. This wasn't fully clear to me until the Covington Catholic boys were pilloried by the mainstream media. They were persecuted because they were white, unapologetic, and conservative - in that order. Anyone with any amount of awareness of leftist identity politics and America's demographic shift at the behest of her political elite could see this.

The usual MAGA conservatives took to their podiums and decried the 'Fake News' of the situation. Clearly, they were in the right to do this. But there was an element missing that only makes sense when you figure some of these people are chasing fame. Their reaction was similar to a middle school leadership class' response to a tragedy like a suicide, "This is bad! We need to raise awareness. We're raising funds. It's time for a bake sale!" No discussion of *why* the kid killed himself or the few willing to go there to some degree are unwilling to discuss the corruption in the family, intergenerational trauma, and a moral indictment of the suicided kid's parents. That would be too close to the pulse of the situation. That would provoke too much discomfort and force a light to shine upon one's own parents and the parents of others in the leadership group. The mood of the bake sale would be soured.

I compared the activist response of many in the MAGA crowd to Stefan Molyneux's response. Stefan initially tweeted out in support. Then he waited a few days and did a comprehensive examination of the libel against the Covington Catholic boys titled, "The Truth About the Covington Confrontation[102]." At one point in the presentation he says:

> It is my absolute desperate desire to find ways to de-escalate but not to the point where whites just have to abandon any kind of survivability in the countries that whites originally created. That is not an option. This is why we're facing a particular challenge. Whites being knights, whites giving way has not de-escalated things but rather has made things worse as appeasement generally does throughout history.... If you're not white, it's hard for you to understand the racism whites are exposed to on a continual basis.

This commentary gets at the heart of racial tensions today. He gets at the 'why' of the situation. As I wrote on January 21st, 2019:

---

[102] https://www.youtube.com/watch?v=tCAgeoXYtkE

No doubt, it is useful to raise awareness and funds, get hashtags trending, talk with the aggrieved but 'Stand with Covington' also means talking about how whites are the group most discriminated against in the USA. THAT gets at the 'why' and reduces the chance of recurrence.

Are we to follow these MAGA conservatives (some call them "free thinkers" or "Alt-Lite") into oblivion while they make little to no effort to raise the ethnic consciousness of whites? Are we to bake sale and defamation lawsuit our way back into firm possession of our ethnic homelands? Perhaps, but I am growing increasingly skeptical.

These people are exposed to the great arguments that Stefan Molyneux makes. Many of them are friends with Molyneux, have appeared in interviews and at events with the man, and retweet him from time to time, particularly when he sticks to palatable topics outside of race and IQ.

Defeating the mainstream media through verbal confrontation and by convincing tech giants to not give the media power is absolutely valid. It is perhaps the center mass in the battle for civilization. But what good are our "influencers" and "opinion makers" if they dislodge legacy media by becoming famous themselves only to deliberately avoid any public sympathy with white racial consciousness? Are they banking on the right "game"? It is still not clear to me. This is an exploration.

Nobody is taking more chances in the public sphere than Stefan Molyneux right now. When he was happy to play the game the free-thinkers were playing, to score zingers on the legacy media, he was the toast of the town. Now some of these people have backed away from him. Maybe I am mistaken here. I cannot posit this with too much certainty and there is certainly no clandestine, coordinated effort on the part of MAGA folks to distance themselves from Molyneux. But at what point are people playing for clicks, retweets, public prestige as a freedom fighter, and networks of financial supporters at the expense of telling the public the most important truths that will help inoculate it against further disaster? Does Stefan Molyneux ever intend to play for clicks by using "persuasion" or does he tell the simple truth and let the consequences play out how they will? I'm inclined to think he pursues the latter, exclusively. He's relaxed about it. He does not try to work others up into a frenzy. He takes his time and speaks when he has clarity. I'm not a mind reader. I'd wager to guess that there is no one he feels he needs his picture taken with. Can the same be said about everyone who came to the aid of the Covington Catholic boys?

After thinking about this some in the week following the Covington Confrontation, I tweeted:

> At some point people are going to feel tired of being treated like lab rats the cool kids practice 'persuasion' on and turn to more plainspoken, earnest platformers like Stefan Molyneux. He doesn't psychologically manipulate people. He's secure in himself.

Why is it so important that my sense of injustice be stoked up to raise money and the profile of persuasive platformers? What's the motive in that? Certainly, some of it is benign and of great good to the world. But strangely it never involves a frank discussion of the intelligence disparities between the races, the importance of white ethnic consciousness, or how heavily the political and social scales are tilted against white in-group preferences. What use are black conservatives to me when they've been shown endless empathy and sympathy for their maltreatment at the hands of Democrats and are unwilling to reciprocate similarly in any explicit terms for the maltreatment whites have endured by other groups? Should I give them my money, encouragement, and attention? Should I 'keep it positive' and enjoy their hip-hop-ization of conservatism? What use will they or their cohorts of other races be to me when the ethnic and sectarian violence they deliberately avoided addressing finally breaks out?

The only way I seem to be able to make sense of this kid glove treatment of MAGA audiences is that it operates much the same way "raising awareness" of suicide never seems to lay moral fault at the feet of abusive parents. Why go there when the retweets and the money are rolling in? There's no need, particularly if you are black, Jewish, Hispanic, or even a white homosexual. You have no "skin in the game" for the white race but you can make plenty of money and fame off of them in the meanwhile.

Of course, I don't think all of these people who tip-toe around race and IQ or a frank discussion of the political in-group strategies of the races are malevolent in their intentions. But I do think they enjoy the quick fame granted to them by hundreds of thousands of conservatives who truly don't want to face how tilted the scales are toward their systematic eradication. The legacy media relayed the bigotry of the masses back to them for decades. It's not a stretch to assume that the very first transitionary period away from legacy, television media would involve some level of bigotry mirroring on the part of those seeking to usurp the legacy media. Part of what is so celebrated about the Zoomer generation, even on the part of these MAGA platformers, is the relative lack of "Boomer conditioning" in the Zoomers. Zoomers, the ones who are honest, show a remarkable lack of need to play to appearances, persuade others with NLP and CBT verbal trickery, or "try to go viral". So many of these young people, who have yet to make their major mark on the world, simply express themselves the way Molyneux does when he's relaxed and on a roll. They're unafraid to go straight into the ugly heart of the matter.

They're racially aware and not in the "Black History Month" manner that public schooling would prefer them to be.

Immigration patriots in the vein of Nick Fuentes, Faith Goldy, Lauren Rose, Jesse Lee Peterson, Ann Coulter, VDare, Scott Greer, and others, who are certainly distinguished and apart from the "MAGA free thinker" crowd, possess an earnestness about race relations that is refreshing. While there is an acceptance on the part of these people that America *has* become a multicultural society, by sheer force of demographics, there is not even tacit approval or sanction of this situation. These people have standards and a preference to associate with other small government minded, white, and heterosexual people. There is no hostility toward other groups. But nor is there any attempt made to "score zingers" on Christianity or lecture Christians about how Muslims are sometimes nicer on Twitter. These people talk about *why* whites are under duress, both from their own making and from out-group pressures. These people, along with Molyneux who is in his own camp, tell it like it is. They understand how dire the situation is while keeping their messaging universalist and accessible to anyone reasonably proud of their own roots.

I want de-escalation just like anyone remotely in the MAGA world. But I don't want the hedging, kumbaya awareness-raising from people with no skin in the game: biological white children of their own. These are people who mix in grandiose statements about themselves into their cultural and current events commentary in order to try to stoke my insecurities so I will unconsciously position them as an authority over my own understanding of the situation. I want to listen to people who understand just how dire the situation is, are willing to state it, and are unwilling to alter their personalities so as to draw less violence on themselves when tensions finally explode. I want to listen to and relate with people who are risking it all, not giving half or three-quarters truths in order to amass plentiful resources in an effort to compensate for some childhood deficit of attention and intellectual validation.

I'm happy to help MAGA folks, or people from whatever form of conservative populism is on the horizon, but I will not suspend my understanding of the deeper dynamics at play for their benefit. Sometimes they treat me as bitter, cynical, or even a persona non grata. How dare I not fall head over heels for a white free thinker's attempts at rebranding himself as a rapper since he's unwilling to be self-knowledgeable! I'm supposed to support and encourage unconditionally! That's hating, not creating - they assert. Personally, I think I'm skeptical, aware of the impending violence, and willing to help these people up to a point. I think it is *they* who are bitter, cynical, and unwilling to give themselves to the cause of helping whites to have in-group preferences and some measure of spine in their own homelands, despite knowing better. They are non-whites or have non-white children and operate in what they think is a meritocracy of skill but is in fact a distortion field created by government control of demographics. It is they who try to convince others that reality is, in fact, a simulation. They can't imagine they're playing themselves since, after all, they receive endless well-wishes, clicks and retweets, and bias confirmation on a daily basis. They're surrounded by supporters who nurture their shared delusions, not haters who would pop their denial bubbles. And these platformers are genuinely effective to a degree, which buys them space to operate – and rightfully so. It's not all inauthentic.

In some ways, I think these people stand in the way. Some of them even quietly know they're wrong and will admit the importance of race and IQ in private. I'm sure there are a lot of people who more or less have the perspective I've named in this essay. There are more and more of us, as the objective evidence points in a certain direction, who feel a lot of frustration at offering these people accurate corrections and rebuttals over Twitter and receiving absolutely no response. I just don't give these "free thinking" people direct attention anymore. Every now and then they float into my periphery because they say something valid and useful to my cause and I will retweet them. Check my timeline. They're there. I don't want a hostile relationship with these people. I downright love some of them. But I can't pretend that most of them are unwilling to respond to reason and evidence beyond a certain point and that this isn't a grating personality defect on their part. I'm not perfect. I know I need to "create not hate". I'm simply unwilling to imbue my creations with half measures and false sentiments. I'm not going to pretend to be a MAGA rapper. That's not my heritage. I have plenty of music online. Five or six albums, in fact. I have around 350 videos on YouTube. I have written several books. I just can't pretend it's not as bad as it is and that we have a lot more time than we actually do. I can't pretend I like Kanye West as a person or an artist simply because he supports Donald Trump and MAGA. I have sympathy for his values, but he is not familial to me. He's also got a bit of an anti-white streak. And so does virtually anyone else who went through public schooling and doesn't have skin in the game. I won't pretend this isn't the case.

This is an essay about differentiation, not condemnation. I am happy "free thinkers" exist, relative to most of the people on the planet. I share a lot of their values. I think they throw great parties. But we do not share the value of "be totally honest as the truth is revealed to you". I know very well many of these people have been exposed to philosophical arguments made by Stefan Molyneux on race, IQ, and ethnic consciousness. Nary a peep! I won't accept that as my standard. I haven't erected my life in such a manner that forthrightness on these topics would earn me intellectual ostracism by my fellow platformers. The same can't be said about Owen Benjamin but he's gone on right ahead and done the right thing, to share the truth as it has occurred to him. He was immediately booted from "the Intellectual Dark Web" and no "free thinker" has tried to promote his work since he was banned from Twitter. That's not how I roll. Nor is it how you have to roll.

Male Bonding

A friendship between men can remake whole societies and often has throughout world history. Deeper male bonding is shouted down by the establishment for a wide variety of reasons, the foremost being that men who are loyal to one another cannot be bought out. The establishment thrives on sellouts. Men of great talent and skill seek out the fame and glory owed to them and the powers that be are all too happy to elevate them, for a price. A man who is deeply bonded with his fellow man is difficult to dislodge from a morally excellent path. This is why there is a war on fatherhood. Good fatherhood begets men who are capable of uniting with other men in a meaningful fashion. When enough men are united in a righteous cause, it is usually the establishment that comes under attack. Hence, male bonding has been made into a cultural relic.

The television programs dominating the ratings today are almost entirely comprised of women endeavoring to advance their careers, set dramas right, and do silly things like fight crime and kick butt. The men in popular television today are all busy lounging around, being effeminate with one another, sulking as loners, or wearing suits and engaging in criminal activities. Christian television and movies seem to be the only places where men are shown getting along and teaming up to resolve social ills without violence. But Christian messaging is subservient to a foreign power and the moral lessons are watered down. None of the fire and brimstone, hardline spirit of the pre-television Christianity persists.

As Jonathan Bowden discussed, Western cinema has seen the lone vigilante seeking out justice through retribution as the main masculine ideal. This has persisted from the days of Clint Eastwood spaghetti Westerns up to the Batman films of Christopher Nolan. This is an incomplete, inaccurate depiction of masculinity because it conveys the message that one man set apart from the pack is able to catalyze social change through destructive means. This message couldn't possibly be more at odds with reality. With an all pervasive surveillance state, Donald Trump giving out every military weapon and vehicle he possibly can to law enforcement around the country, and a media that has done everything in its power to obscure the sources of social alienation for those rare few who do decide to pursue lone gunman vigilantism, the equation is completely weighted against the vigilante to the point of assured suicide by cop. Yet, the lone vigilante trope persists. The establishment encourages and glorifies it and every now and then a stupid, disaffected young man gives all the social proof the masses will ever need that it is better to stay with the herd. The establishment probably carries out some of these shootings. In this day and age, vigilante films are a way of effectively taunting what little masculinity remains in the population.

Vigilantism is a Third World strategy. Vigilantism is the way of Brazilians, Filipinos, and Pakistanis. It will not lead to greater liberty because it is not politically cohesive. It only leads to more social chaos, despite being depicted as masculine in cinema.

The establishment most fears men who deliberate, organize, hold their ranks, and take over the institutions. Before the Internet, the establishment was able to quash dissent entirely. George S. Patton was assassinated in his hospital bed when a planned car crash didn't do the job. JFK was shot in the most public fashion possible after warning America of a monolithic and ruthless conspiracy. Huey Long was murdered when it looked like he would unseat FDR. Oswald Mosley was locked up for the duration of WWII. Rudolf Hess was locked in a tower for 46 years before his suicide was faked. Countless dissidents perished in the Gulag and the Holodomor. Corneliu

Codreanu was murdered for being too well liked by his fellow Romanians. With no Internet to mass proliferate populist messages and document the wellbeing of political dissidents, the central bankers were able to pick off whoever they damn well pleased at any point in time for any reason.

The equation has changed and so long as there is some measure of free speech in the West, political dissidents representing the will of the people will be able to operate freely to a greater extent than possible ever before. Alex Jones can go on Joe Rogan's podcast and tell the world about the elite's plans for a breakaway civilization, how Churchill initiated the targeting of civilians in WWII, and how the world's billionaires fund psychedelic research to try and establish clandestine contact with interdimensional beings. While the truth value of these propositions is open for dispute, the fact that Alex Jones is successfully sewing tremendous distrust toward the ultra-wealthy and powerful in America is not. Jones' great strides are only made more evident by the fact that Apple, Facebook, Twitter, the major credit card companies, and YouTube have all deplatformed him. The courts have tried to separate him from his children. The man is pinned to the wall by the powers that be for telling the world the Chinese are running tissue farms for life extension technologies for the elite. Still he thrashes and makes war. Countless men have been murdered or sent to death camps for saying far less.

As stated earlier in this book, masculinity has to do with fatherhood and the virtuous continuation of Western Civilization against all evils. We owe it to the men who have bled and sacrificed to give us the freedoms we enjoy today to band together and depose the Satanic cabal at the heart of organized society. This grand scheme starts with friendship between men. Friendship between men takes patience to wade through the gobs and gobs of bad programming instilled in young men for the past three generations. There's plenty of nihilism, feminism, laziness, entitlement, and masochism for young men to clean out of their systems. The technocratic fascists want for modern men to look and act like the bug boys from Big Bang Theory. Not only should men look and act like bugs, they should be eating bugs too:

> World population is slated to top nine billion by 2050 and seeing as how arable land is being rapidly swallowed by towns and cities, oceans are increasingly overfished, and climate change is disrupting traditional farming, a new United Nations study proposes a twist on Marie Antoinette's dietary advice: let them eat bugs.[103]

Beyond Meat, a food company that wants to fool consumers into thinking they're eating meat by approximating the tactile experience through a variety of techniques using plant-based proteins raised $183 million as of 2015[104] with at least $55 million since then by globalist stalwarts like Bill Gates, Tyson Foods, Leonardo DiCaprio, and various Democrat NBA players[105]. The American Psychological Association, which was infiltrated and taken over by gay rights activists in the 1970's who proceeded to change guidelines on homosexuality despite the longstanding literature[106], has also entered the fray. The massively influential organization has put "toxic masculinity" squarely in its crosshairs by changing treatment guidelines once again for the sake of political correctness:

---

[103] https://www.theregister.co.uk/2013/05/13/insects_as_food_and_feed/
[104] https://agfundernews.com/beyond-meat-raising-series-e-round-obvious-ventures-invests-17m-so-far4872.html
[105] https://www.nbcsports.com/boston/celtics/kyrie-irvings-vegan-venture-celtics-star-featured-beyond-meats-ad
[106] Satinover, J. (1998). Homosexuality and the politics of truth. Grand Rapids, MI: Baker Books.

> The guidelines support encouraging positive aspects of "traditional masculinity," such as courage & leadership, and discarding traits such as violence & sexism, while noting that the vast majority of men are not violent. Traits of so-called "traditional masculinity," like suppressing emotions & masking distress, often start early in life & have been linked to less willingness by boys & men to seek help, more risk-taking & aggression -- possibly harming themselves & those with whom they interact.[107]

Heaven forbid men take any risks in order to act in a violent manner toward evil-doers! There are no evil-doers in a post-modern society and the establishment enshrined "philosophers" of the day keep their sweet book deals by feigning ignorance of the possibility that there may be some way of establishing secular ethics throughout society. Men are to be bug consuming soy nerds who have to be nice all the time and accept whatever is tossed in the trough for them by the beautiful faces on the screens. Never mind the child blood drinkers lurking in the distant background, sipping margaritas on Lolita Island and sacrificing the economic futures of the last remaining free peoples through debt schemes and money printing.

Vegan, consumerist men will never depose the evil powers that be. Therefore, all men must be made into consumerist veganistas! This is not only limited to white men. More black men in dresses show up to the Oscars these days than black men wearing suits. Every black man earning over a certain threshold in Hollywood's sick industry is made to wear a dress. The higher they go, the more denigrating the public rituals of humiliation. The elite know that Muslim men can be corrupted as well, given the high rates of boy rape

---

[107] https://www.rt.com/usa/448410-apa-masculinity-bad-psychology/

among the oil rich sheikhs who run the Middle East. All will be made sexually deviant, plant and bug eaters.

A young man seeking fraternity needs patience to wade through all the bad programming. The bad programming never ends. Young men who form true bonds must live in a conspiracy against this bad programming. They must reject it, converse in private away from their devices, make assurances for their income and familial prospects, and maintain a state of preparedness for the converging catastrophes. This ethos is subversive. The establishment labels it "fascism" but it is not. The natural way of things has always involved men working together. These men have always eaten meat. They have always taken risks and employed violence when under attack. The establishment wants for every righteous situation of self-defense against tyranny to be reframed psychologically as oppositional defiant disorder whereupon medications are prescribed, men and boys are incarcerated, and fraternal bonds are broken altogether. Righteous anger must be recast as "vindictiveness". Resistance to the Great Mother of the state is always and forever naughty and worthy of a visit from the multicultural police force administrating the shopping zone the dissident male finds himself in.

Fraternal bonds are worth pursuing. Intellectual discourse at great length makes for the most satisfying, bond-strengthening experience a person can engage in. There is no friendship quite like sharing in the development of another man's genius. Men have always been capable of destroying one another in hand to hand combat, so they have turned to highly conceptual systems of ethics and thought in order to resolve their differences. Tribal, communal, and national ties have been formed through countless discussions through the night by the best stock the human species has been capable of bringing to bear.

Diaspora Mindset

Diaspora is defined as people settled far from their ancestral homelands, the place where these people live, and the movement, migration, or scattering of a people away from an established or ancestral homeland. The online dictionary sites are quick to offer up Africans taken from Africa during the Trans-Atlantic slave trade. Jews, whites, and blacks who ran the Trans-Atlantic slave trade weren't even the largest proprietors of African slavery:

> Thomas Sowell [Thomas Sowell, Race and Culture, BasicBooks, 1994, p. 188] estimates that 11 million slaves were shipped across the Atlantic and 14 million were sent to the Islamic nations of North Africa and the Middle East.[108]

A more honest example would be the whites taken from Europe by Muslim slave traders from the 1300's to early 1700's:

> It is estimated that up to 1.25 million Europeans were enslaved by the so-called Barbary corsairs, and their lives were just as pitiful as their African counterparts. They have come to be known as the white slaves of Barbary.[109]

Even a liberal source like PBS can only pin African slave numbers in America at 388,000[110]. Nor were the Muslim slave raiders content to operate just on the Barbary Coast, as has been popularized by the few

---

[108] https://www.politicalislam.com/tears-of-jihad/
[109] https://www.ancient-origins.net/ancient-places-africa/white-slaves-barbary-002171
[110] https://www.pbs.org/wnet/african-americans-many-rivers-to-cross/history/how-many-slaves-landed-in-the-us/

historians who are even willing to acknowledge mass enslavement of whites:

> However, not content with attacking ships and sailors, the corsairs also sometimes raided coastal settlements in Italy, France, Spain, Portugal, England, Ireland, and even as far away as the Netherlands and Iceland. They landed on unguarded beaches and crept up on villages in the dark to capture their victims. Almost all the inhabitants of the village of Baltimore, in Ireland, were taken in this way in 1631.

Enslaved whites were scattered to the wind in the Middle Ages and early Renaissance. The virtual lack of traceable Arab-White admixture in the genetic features of the modern-day Middle Easterner sheds insight into what happened to those 1.25 million plus Europeans who were stolen from their homelands: the men were all castrated or murdered. Black slaves in America received far better treatment and their ancestors have prominent roles in American society today.

We'll dig more into the myth of white guilt in a moment.

Whites have been a diaspora before, they may become a diaspora again. The French will likely be the first to be expelled from their homelands:

> The number below is the percentage of baby names that seem Islamic. A cautious approach was taken when deciding whether a name was Islamic or not: if there was any ambiguity, it was not included in the figures. Thus, the actual rate of islamisation is probably higher than is revealed by

these figures. Nationally, around 18% of babies in France are now being given Islamic forenames.[111]

Eighteen percent being a conservative estimate. The French brought us post-modernist philosopher Michel Foucault, famous for dying of AIDS, who petitioned his government to lower the age of consent so he could have sex with boys[112] and spread his AIDS to boys at homosexual bathhouses[113] stating, "Besides, to die for the love of boys: what could be more beautiful?[114]" The French adored their philosopher, who picked up quite the reputation when he taught at Berkeley, "where he was known among students of the day as "that mad French leather queen who whips anyone who'll let him at San Francisco gay bath houses." America produced Ayn Rand. France produced Michel Foucault in the same period.

The gentle Swedes are hot in tow, with 20.1% of their population being foreign born in 2012[115] prior to the European migrant crisis. Peter Imanuelsen, a colleague of mine known as PeterSweden, writes in The Gateway Pundit:

> A billboard featuring a woman in hijab welcoming motorists to the Swedish city of Gävle has caused outrage on social media.

---

[111] https://diversitymachtfrei.wordpress.com/2017/01/08/the-islamisation-of-france-as-revealed-by-baby-names/

[112] https://en.wikipedia.org/wiki/French_petition_against_age_of_consent_laws

[113] https://www.newcriterion.com/issues/1993/3/the-perversions-of-m-foucault

[114] https://philosophynow.org/issues/65/Philosophers_Behaving_Badly_by_Nigel_Rodgers_and_Mel_Thompson

[115] http://worldpopulationreview.com/countries/sweden-population/

It turns out that the woman on the billboard named Suzan Hindi has connections to a Salafist extremist Mosque which has urged followers to donate money to support terrorism – And now this woman is one of the people featured to represent the Swedish city! The Al-Rashideen Mosque in Gävle has a long history of extremism. A Qatari organisation bought a Methodist church and changed it into the Mosque. One of the founders of the same organisation, Abd al-Rahman bin Umayr al-Nuaymi was revealed to have been one of the biggest financiers of Al-Qaeda in Iraq, which later turned into ISIS. The man has since 2013 been on the terror list of the US, EU and UN.[116]

Parts of Sweden are openly Islamic now. Islam has this interesting clause in the doctrine where non-believers must be put to death and has waged total war on various civilizations for the past 1400 years. Estimated numbers of non-believers put to death by Islamists are[117]:

-120 million Africans

-60 million Christians

-80 million Hindus

-10 million Buddhists

-tens of thousands of Jews

It is not difficult to surmise what will happen to the ethnic Swedish population of ~8 million as jihadists take more and more political

---

[116] https://www.thegatewaypundit.com/2019/02/official-swedish-welcome-sign-to-city-of-gavle-features-woman-in-hijab-with-connections-to-isis-mosque/

[117] https://www.politicalislam.com/tears-of-jihad/

power, operating more and more openly to spread their doctrine of wanton destruction and global domination. But enough about Islam, let's talk about the Jews!

The Jewish people are relevant to our discussion of a white diaspora because of their longstanding status as a diaspora, in particular prior to the formation of the nation state of Israel in 1948. Estimates vary but Jews have been expelled from at least 109 locations or countries since 250 A.D.[118] The Jews know about maintaining international movement in an effort to survive. Some Jews, like Jared Kushner, are so enamored with movement across international boundaries that, according to Haaretz, are working within government to, "eliminate the borders as they are today, 'in order to guarantee freedom of movement for people and goods.'[119]"

The most popular theory for explaining Jewish intelligence ties in with the Jewish diaspora status. In Ernest van den Haag's *The Jewish Mystique*[120] the case is made that not only were Middle Ages Catholics cloistering away their most intelligent into lives of celibacy while the Jews encouraged their most intelligent to reproduce the most, selective pressures resulting from expulsion favored the Jews who were most fleet with their resources and adroit in interpreting Medieval law for their favor or preservation. The result of at least eight centuries of selective pressures has resulted in a race of people almost an entire standard deviation of intelligence higher at 110-115 IQ than the average European IQ of 97[121]. While the intelligence scores may have been cherrypicked to heavily favor Jews, as Vox Day

---

[118] https://www.biblebelievers.org.au/expelled.htm
[119] (https://www.haaretz.com/israel-news/.premium-kushner-trump-peace-plan-to-address-israel-s-borders-united-palestinian-entity-1.6964706
[120] Haag, E. V. (1977). The Jewish mystique. New York: Stein and Day.
[121] https://aristocratsofthesoul.com/average-iq-by-race-and-ethnicity/

argues[122], Jewish economic success is undeniable. Not only do Jews outperform natives wherever they are granted legal equality, they also form vast networks of association and mutual support because of their emphasis on the concept of "success" as that which serves the Jewish community. The Jews have marvelously strong in-group preferences and strategies that allow them to hold major stakes in banking, finance, media, and lobbying. In an article titled "Jewish Americans Are Now The Face Of Trump Resistance" by The Jerusalem Post we read:

> In midterm elections on Tuesday, 79% of Jewish voters chose Democrats, according to exit polls conducted by Pew Research Center and CNN. Only 17% supported Republicans– down nearly 10% in two short, if eventful years. And they are getting elected. Across the country, 30 Jewish Americans were elected or reelected to the House– only two of which are Republicans– and four to the Senate, just shy of marking record-high Jewish representation on Capitol Hill. Democrats' sole pickup seat from Republicans in the Senate, in Nevada, was Jacky Rosen, formerly president of her synagogue congregation. What, if anything, does their Judaism have to do with their politics? Statistics would suggest quite a bit. A majority of American Jews have voted for progressive candidates and causes in elections since at least 1984, when record-keeping began on Jewish voter patterns, and when roughly 7 in 10 community members began reliably voting Democratic– a direct response to a Republican alignment with evangelical Christians that

---

[122] https://voxday.blogspot.com/2018/04/the-myth-of-jewish-intelligence.html

appeared at the time hostile to Jews and their pluralistic values.[123]

Jews also represent 33% of the Supreme Court, despite being 2% of the population, with Ruth Bader Ginsburg appointed in 1993, Stephen Breyer appointed in 1994, and Elena Kagan appointed in 2010. All three Justices were Democrat appointees[124]. Jewish political and economic power is evident across America's institutions and America's Silent Majority stands to learn a lesson. Perhaps a diaspora mindset is in order. Let's examine the components of a diaspora mindset.

No Collective Guilt Admitted, No Apologies

Another word or two here on the myth of collective guilt for whites over the institution of slavery.

The basic standpoint of left-wing crybullies concerning slavery is that blacks are owed reparations by whites for slavery of blacks in the 18th and 19th centuries. It boils down to a money grab. They explain income differences between blacks and whites by saying there's "systemic racism", rather than pointing to IQ differences. Since there's "racism" embedded within the system itself, it's time whites fork over even more cash than they already have to try and close the income gap. Ta-Nehisi Coates writes in her piece for The Atlantic titled *The Case for Reparations*:

---

[123] https://www.jpost.com/Diaspora/Jewish-Americans-are-now-the-face-of-Trump-resistance-571399

[124] https://en.wikipedia.org/wiki/Demographics_of_the_Supreme_Court_of_the_United_States#Jewish_justices

> Black families, regardless of income, are significantly less wealthy than white families. The Pew Research Center estimates that white households are worth roughly 20 times as much as black households, and that whereas only 15 percent of whites have zero or negative wealth, more than a third of blacks do. Effectively, the black family in America is working without a safety net.[125]

The solution?

> Reparations—by which I mean the full acceptance of our collective biography and its consequences—is the price we must pay to see ourselves squarely. What I'm talking about is more than recompense for past injustices—more than a handout, a payoff, hush money, or a reluctant bribe. What I'm talking about is a national reckoning that would lead to spiritual renewal.

The "all modern-day white Americans are guilty for the slavery of blacks in the USA that ended 152 years ago and thus owe a tremendous moral and economic debt" point of view is as full of holes as a block of Swiss cheese. This toxic myth is easily defeated yet it persists in the minds of millions of Americans. Until it is overwhelmingly defeated, this myth will continue to erode any positive sense of ethnic unity among whites. Let's take a closer look at the holes in the cheese.

The first basic problem with "muh slavery reparations" is that black Africans captured and sold into slavery their own brethren. The Constitutional Rights Foundation tells us that:

---

[125] https://www.theatlantic.com/magazine/archive/2014/06/the-case-for-reparations/361631/)

> Local African rulers and black merchants delivered captured people to these trading posts to sell as slaves to European ship captains. About 50 percent of the slaves were taken as prisoners during the frequent tribal wars occurring among the West African kingdoms. Another 30 percent became slaves as punishment for crimes or indebtedness. The remainder were kidnapped by black slave traders.[126]

Uh oh! Do the descendants of tribal leaders in Sierra Leone owe Bill Cosby, Condoleezza Rice, Al Sharpton, Michelle Obama, and Samuel L. Jackson millions of dollars in reparations[127]? That's a pretty huge stab in the back, money or no money offered, to hunt down and trap your ethnic brethren to sell to slavers. It's a level of barbarity we cannot fathom today. Can you imagine looking out your window and seeing your neighbor's house under siege because it was decided they needed to be put on spaceships to Mars to work the spice mines? At least the technology would have advanced beyond spears and iron chains.

In this left-wing world of, "Apologize for things people did hundreds of years ago" even the Nigerians themselves are jumping in to demand apologies. The Civil Rights Congress of Nigeria stated in 2009 that:

> In view of the fact that the Americans and Europe have accepted the cruelty of their roles and have forcefully apologised, it would be logical, reasonable and humbling if African traditional rulers ... [can] accept blame and formally

---

[126] http://www.crf-usa.org/black-history-month/the-slave-trade
[127] (https://www.therichest.com/rich-list/most-influential/5-influential-americans-with-slave-ancestry/

apologise to the descendants of the victims of their collaborative and exploitative slave trade.[128]

Had these African chiefs never sold out their tribal and intertribal brethren, the institution of slavery could not have persisted on the North American continent as it did.

The next basic problem with the racial demagoguery of the left is that at the height of American slavery, made possible by African treason, about 1 to 2 percent of Americans owned slaves[129]. The rate can be nudged up to 5 percent[130] since trying to Google statistics on race, intelligence, or slavery now just cascades you with social justice warrior websites such as TheRoot.com telling you what a bad white person you've been. Google is run by SJWs and wrongthink is not allowed. Since such a small percentage of the white population of the United States owned slaves during the institution of slavery, why exactly should whites who were not descended from these people pony up reparation money and public displays of guilt? We could dredge up the mental gymnastics leftists go into about "collective guilt" at this point but let's save ourselves the social justice lobotomy. There's no rational answer for this that has ever made any headway in the free market.

Looking more closely, we also find out that, "The statistics show that, when free, blacks disproportionately became slave masters.[131][132]" Let's not forget that these people were only a ship ride removed from an atmosphere of horrid African treachery and racial

---

[128] https://www.theguardian.com/world/2009/nov/18/africans-apologise-slave-trade
[129] http://www.civil-war.net/pages/1860_census.html
[130] http://spartacus-educational.com/USAsownership.htm
[131] https://americancivilwar.com/authors/black_slaveowners.htm
[132] https://www.census.gov/prod/www/decennial.html#y1860

treason. 28 percent of freed black slaves owned slaves. This is a far higher percentage than white slave ownership, even if we adjust for social justice magic math.

Another kicker to the welfare grabs of the left is that hundreds upon hundreds of thousands of Irish (white people) were transported to the Americas as slaves[133]. At one point, a British ship crew dumped 1,302 Irish slaves overboard so that the crew would have enough food to eat. Irish slaves were treated as much more expendable than African slaves and came at a lower cost. Irish population in the 1600's dropped from 1,500,000 to 600,000 due to British enslavement. One could consider this genocide, and at a far more extensive scale than total African suffering, which was catalyzed by African to African enslavement. White slaves in America during the 1600's outnumbered black slaves. If currently aggrieved African-Americans want to ensure reparations are shared around justly, perhaps they should send money to Ireland. This would be a sign of good faith.

One more "hate fact" to add onto the fire here: only 4.4% of slaves transferred across the Atlantic between 1450 and 1900 actually went to America. The vast majority of them, 35.4% went to Brazil.[134] There are so many descendants of slaves in Brazil that one could almost consider the nation itself to be one giant reparation for slaves. Or, it could be that Brazil and Portugal owe descendants of Irish slaves reparation money in excess to the proportion allotted for aggrieved African Americans since Irish slaves were treated unequally by being given lower price tags. There's some social justice magic math for you. For the left, leaving cities such as NYC, Chicago, and Los Angeles to go pester Portuguese and Brazilians about reparations

---

[133] http://www.globalresearch.ca/the-irish-slave-trade-the-forgotten-white-slaves/31076
[134] http://logicalmeme.com/?p=3188

isn't as appealing as staying in the comfort of one's own apartment writing aggrievement blog posts directed at conservative whites. American public schooling, paid for by property-owning taxpayers, taught these racial demagogues English. It's English they'll have to use to try and prey upon white guilt.

With potentially explosive implications, if we are to buy into the myth of collective guilt, it is worth noting that the major slave transporting ships of the era were actually owned by Asiatic Jews. Rabbi Marc Lee Raphael writes:

> In Curacao in the seventeenth century, as well as in the British colonies of Barbados and Jamaica in the eighteenth century, Jewish merchants played a major role in the slave trade. In fact, in all the American colonies, whether French (Martinique), British, or Dutch, Jewish merchants frequently dominated.[135]

Jews were so far involved in the Dutch slave trade that trading was suspended on Jewish holidays. Looks like those wanting reparations are going to have to book plane tickets to Israel, as well.

It is estimated that 1.3 million whites were taken as slaves to North Africa as part of the Muslim-led Barbary slave trade[136]. This is about a tenth of the total number of Africans taken from Africa, by African captors and Jewish ships, to the Western Hemisphere. Should social justice warriors demanding reparations include a 10% discount on top of the Irish discount rate they ought to have factored in already

---

[135] http://12160.info/forum/topics/jewish-slave-ship-owners?xg_source=activity

[136] http://www.bbc.co.uk/history/british/empire_seapower/white_slaves_01.shtml

by now? The myth of slavery reparations is looking thoroughly haggard and debunked about now. As this mummy stumbles and falls, let's kick it in the nads one more time. US Representative Steve King writes:

> Confirmed in "Christian Slaves, Muslim Masters" by Robert C. Davis-Ohio State University. As many as 1,250,000 whites enslaved by Muslims while 600,000 black Africans were enslaved in what is now the U.S. 600,000 white Americans lost their lives in the struggle to end slavery.[137]

Robert Davis doesn't his numbers quite right. There were 800,000 men who died in the Civil War. It's fair to say that instead of tearing down Confederate monuments in the South, social justice warriors should be erecting alongside them monuments of a different order. More respect should be shown to all the white men who gave their lives to once and for all settle the question of whether there would be slavery institutionalized in the West. If anything, there should be more *Union* memorials everywhere in the South.

Buddhists didn't lift a finger to end slavery in the West. They get to keep their temples and monuments.

Muslims continue to propagate slavery by the tens of thousands, making all manner of sex slaves out of little white girls in the UK. The European Union is actually demolishing churches to make way for their mosques.

Whites? Well, it seems they're just bad no matter what good they do.

If the basic principle to extract from those who demand slavery reparations is the idea that all white people are accountable for the actions of 1-2% of white Americans 150 years ago, we can then say

---

[137] https://twitter.com/SteveKingIA/status/932083079426007040

that all current blacks are accountable for the actions of a few criminals a hundred years ago. That's racist as hell. It's well and understood as racism when minorities are unfairly collectivized but when it's done to whites it's be lauded and rewarded with mainstream media coverage. Fortunately, the world can't run on falsehoods for long at all.

"It is only racist when white people do it" is such a blatant double standard that anyone with half a brain leftover from public schooling can figure it out while they're picking their nose. Double standards are coming to an end. If we're all human beings, standards for ethics must be applied universally. People of color aren't given a "get out of jail free" card simply because their skin is a few shades darker and they were enslaved at lower rates than Irish were 350 years ago.

O.J. Simpson is guilty of a dozen weapons, robbery, and kidnapping charges and was sentenced at one point to 33 years in prison[138]. Are all black people guilty of his criminal charges? Of course not! If time is the only variable that matters in social justice warrior calculations of justice, are all Jews to blame for Jesus' death? Are all Muslims to blame for the rape and slaughter of Spaniards by Moors? Are all Nordics to blame for the slaughter of Frenchmen? Of course not! What if dolphins are a species that understands ethics? Are then all dolphins to blame for the abuse of some shark somewhere at some point in time? Will the little fish ever get their reparations? Maybe!

The simple fact of the matter is that all standards for reparations posited by the left inevitably fail under scrutiny. This is why left wing talk radio is so boring: you can't speak coherently for

---

[138] http://www.vulture.com/2016/01/oj-simpson-crimes-misdemeanors-timeline.html

any period of time when you're not guided by rationally consistent principles. The left has to speak in soundbites or hide their basics premises under mountains of words. People are getting so fed up with the soundbites that even Democrat Beto O'Rourke's own fans are challenging him directly at his rallies, asking, "When am I going to get an actual policy from you instead of platitudes and nice stories?[139]"

White people ended slavery. If the principle to extract from this basic observation of reality is that those who end bad things should be castigated because the good they've done is recast by Democrats as evil, ought we not then send a mob of angry people to kill anyone who does good things? Whoops! That's a bit too close to the truth now, isn't it? Paints a picture of some kind of Communist revolution of some kind where millions of people died from roving mobs of angry people.

Slavery has existed for anywhere from 11,000 to 150,000 years[140]. White people end it and to ensure its ended elsewhere and they are rewarded with calls for them to give up all their money, give up their countries, and have less children. White people end slavery and they then get blamed exclusively for slavery.

The industrial revolution grew only as the institution of slavery ended. Slave owners were not incentivized toward mechanization because it would reduce the value of their slaves. With slavery gone, legally and morally, industrialization happened. Industrialization has led to technology. Technology allows for reparations shysters to spread their toxic message and extract something for nothing. Thankfully, efforts at reparations have largely fallen flat thus far. Yet, this has not stopped 2020 Democratic presidential hopefuls from going back to the old race racket:

---

[139] https://twitter.com/RealSaavedra/status/1108073594280538112
[140] https://en.wikipedia.org/wiki/History_of_slavery

> Massachusetts Sen. Elizabeth Warren, former Housing and Urban Development Secretary Julian Castro, New Jersey Sen. Cory Booker, California Sen. Kamala Harris and author Marianne Williamson have all in some way said they are in favor of reparations for African-Americans — providing compensation to people hurt by discriminatory policies like slavery, Jim Crow laws and redlining. Warren has added that Native Americans should be a part of the conversation, as well.[141]

There's a huge swath of humanity that has developed verbal abilities to extract resources from guilt-ridden people. The longer whites believe they are guilty, the worse it will get for whites.

Whites have nothing to apologize for, whatsoever. The Jews don't apologize for their territorial expansion into formerly Palestinian held lands. The Jews don't apologize for leaving most of the rest of American racial groups in the dust in terms of Democratic voting rates. Whites will need to learn from this example. No white person who is alive is responsible for slavery, colonialism, the massacre of whites by Plains Indians which has been revised to "whites took their lands", or any other historical prejudice the lazy research of the race grifters on the left has revealed.

Whites found functional, capitalist societies with incredible standards of living and opportunity for upward mobility. The rest of the world pours in, demanding whites self-flagellate and give away all their wealth in white genocide schemes like the Green New Deal. It's

---

[141] https://www.npr.org/2019/03/01/698916063/2020-democrats-wrestle-with-a-big-question-what-are-reparations

about time whites stopped this madness and, in fact, expected some gratitude in return for their tremendous tolerance and patience.

Whites need never apologize.

Racial Identity

White identity hasn't been a concept up until the last 120 years, but whites have always been a distinct race, separate from the other races of the world. Nihilists and closeted liberals, not to mention the liberals themselves, are quick to confuse this distinction and say that since white identity is a relatively new phenomena (they'll say it's only 20-30 years old), whites cannot be considered a race. This simply isn't true. Ask any person on the street to distinguish a white person from a non-white person and they will do so with remarkable accuracy, wavering only on Greeks, some Persians, and southern Italians. Whiteness is a quality as distinguishable as the different colored leaves on a tree. Besides, it's hateful to prevent peaceful people from coming up with something new that comes at the expense of no one else. White people get to self-identify, regardless of what an Internet nihilist tweets out.

The Jews have a lovely racial identity that also invokes cultural and religious elements. Though the religious and cultural elements may play the overarching roles in Jewish identity, the genetic component is not eschewed:

> Although he readily acknowledges the formative role of culture and environment, (Harry) Ostrer believes that Jewish identity has multiple threads, including DNA. He offers a

cogent, scientifically based review of the evidence, which serves as a model of scientific restraint.

"On the one hand, the study of Jewish genetics might be viewed as an elitist effort, promoting a certain genetic view of Jewish superiority," he writes. "On the other, it might provide fodder for anti-Semitism by providing evidence of a genetic basis for undesirable traits that are present among some Jews. These issues will newly challenge the liberal view that humans are created equal but with genetic liabilities.[142]"

Jews, he notes, are one of the most distinctive population groups in the world because of our history of endogamy. Jews — Ashkenazim in particular — are relatively homogeneous despite the fact that they are spread throughout Europe and have since immigrated to the Americas and back to Israel. The Inquisition shattered Sephardi Jewry, leading to far more incidences of intermarriage and to a less distinctive DNA.

Dead West Walking argues for whites to have their rightful place in the rich tapestry of human biodiversity, much the same it would have argued for Tutsi preservation had it been written during the Rwandan genocide or for Indian preservation during the Islamic invasion and genocide of 80 million Hindus. Whites get to exist peaceably alongside all the other peoples of the globe. The Jews have understood this about themselves for a long, long time. Their understanding of this principle came into its own during the First Zionist Congress, held in Basel in 1897.

Racial identity for whites does not mean supremacism. It simply means self-assertion. The liberal media is dishonest about

---

[142] https://forward.com/culture/155742/jews-are-a-race-genes-reveal/

anyone who dares explicitly express even a sliver of white racial identity. Something so casual and innocent as, "Through the post-WWII era, whites were responsible for 95% of all scientific advances in the world," draws out every racist Lilliputian the media can mobilize. Whites are not allowed to exist as a distinct race, even by centrists who speak out for free speech but neglect to mention that free speech and common law are distinctly white, European institutions. No dishonest person can admit whites are a separate racial category, despite this being common knowledge before and just after WWI, because the moment this happens the person loses their access to all manner of financial resources arrayed against the existence of whites. Whites not only have one of the higher IQ's among the races, whites also have an independent fighting streak in them that allows for political freedom. The global elite planning their breakaway civilization need a docile, dumb population to extract taxes and devotion from in order to keep their schemes afloat. GDP is the bottom line. International political bodies are used to override any independent schemes and notions whites may have for themselves in their homelands. Whites must be subsumed in a grand, hypersexualized miscegenating process into what Jewish celebrity chef Anthony Bourdain termed a "cappuccino colored people". This is the final solution. Any opposition to multiracialism, which results in multilegalism and an overarching deep state to administrate sectarian squabbles while quietly funneling more money into the pockets of the elite, is termed "racist". Simply disagreeing with Anthony Bourdain's bigotry is a "racist" act, in the new world paradigm.

Nor is modern conservatism without its enemies within. Plenty of political grifters in Conservatism, Inc. and MAGA, Inc. are all too eager to deny whites their existence as a separate category. They use the same nihilistic talking points of centrists and closeted liberals like Jordan Peterson to say, "What is white anyway?" Rather than propose anything themselves, these grifters seek to deconstruct the assertions of others. This results in conferences like CPAC turning into grifter trade shows marked by yarmulkes and the conservative pundit class firmly in the pockets of the foreign labor loving Koch Brothers. Grifters like Sebastian Gorka try to cheerlead Donald Trump into war with Syria and then have the chutzpah to host a show named "America First." Sycophants like Charlie Kirk make healthy livings declaring, "brilliance!" in the wake of Trump's move to sign a spending bill giving defacto amnesty to the entirety of illegal aliens in America. The sad fact of concentrating so much political power into the Executive Branch has resulted in a Norman Peale-positive-thinker like Trump who can be manipulated into any manner of anti-American policy so long as it is presented in positive! terms. The operating strategy for Never Trump staff in the White House has become, "Get Ivanka to throw a tantrum and Jared to yell at someone and the President will sign off on it immediately." Only major outcries by the Silent Majority catch the ear of the President. Otherwise, he is shrouded by people-pleasers and Beltway types who are aligned with the Big Business wing of the GOP.

Minorities of every stripe are allowed to self-identify. TPUSA, a prominent organization on the right, hosts every racial denomination of leadership summit: Young Latino Leaders, Young Black Leaders, etc. To host a Young White Leaders Summit would result in strafing runs from FBI helicopters and ANTIFA pipe bombs under every conference room table. Not to mention, TPUSA's leadership couldn't possibly be bothered to explicitly advocate for whites even if the tables weren't tilted against whites like they are. Their apathy wears a "brilliant!" smile. Sure, they do great by minorities, but it doesn't get to the heart of the matter – as I covered in the section on fame chasers.

The National Council of La Raza, a race-based Hispanic organization, has countless chapters across American universities - every one of them committed to the political and geographic displacement of whites in the western United States. The SPLC and ACLU were founded to politically, financially, and politically dispossess whites and have succeeded over the decades in lawfare to the tune of hundreds of millions of dollars.

The push to blot out any semblance of white identity continues almost totally unabated. Kind of makes you wonder what wonderful things whites could accomplish if they simply had a bit of self-assertion built into their institutions...

National Pride

Poland is doing a lot of things right these days:

Poland's new conservative rulers think their country faces an image problem abroad and they want Hollywood to produce a Polish equivalent of "Braveheart" or "Pearl Harbor" to promote their country's positive place in history. They believe a major movie would make Poland feel proud of its achievements and win it more respect on the world stage at a time when many citizens are falling behind financially. Critics say the government wants to exploit growing feelings of nationalism in order to boost its popularity and divert public attention from economic problems.[143]

---

[143] https://static1.businessinsider.com/r-polish-conservatives-plan-patriotic-hollywood-film-to-boost-image-2015-12

The Poles feel so strongly about their nation that the Polish National Foundation risked international ostracism in order to hire Mel Gibson to star in a commercial celebrating 100 years of Poland regaining independence. Mel Gibson's monologue reads:

> Some say the world is a book but if you don't travel, you'll be on the first page. Like finishing a good book, the most gratifying part of a long journey is coming home. Sometimes it's a fleeting moment or one deep breath. An hour passes. Another hour. Other times it's five hours, six, or ten. Days and nights pass. Sometimes it feels like it's been weeks. Now imagine your journey home lasts 123 years. The Poles didn't have their home for 123 years. Now, a hundred years have passed since they regained their home. Let's celebrate with them.[144]

Poland also hired Liam Neeson in 2018, who recently came under fire for, "(revealing) how he walked the streets with a weapon looking for a 'black bastard' to kill after a loved one 'was raped' as he is branded a 'racist' who 'should be banned from Oscars'.[145]" Poland does not apologize. Nor should it ever have to.

The Poles have such a powerful national pride and identity that philosopher Stefan Molyneux was moved to tears during a national parade in his documentary *The 100 Year March: A Philosopher in Poland*. 200,000 people marched through Warsaw to celebrate 100 years of independence in Poland. The streets were filled to the brim with Polish patriots waving flags, singing national songs,

---

[144] https://www.youtube.com/watch?v=Z57Uuwt1cIk
[145] https://www.dailymail.co.uk/tvshowbiz/article-6665897/Liam-Neeson-reveals-walked-streets-weapon-looking-black-b-d-kill.html

and waving red flares in the air. After decades of committed, dispassionate individualism, Stefan Molyneux confessed:

> I also wanted to put my individualism to the test because those of you who have watched my show for the last 12 years know that I am a very staunch individualist, know that I am skeptical if not hostile to collectivism as a whole and here you can see people marching in the same direction, carrying the same flag with the same pride. And I have to tell you, I feel like something has just kind of broken in two within me. That Aristotle said 2500 years ago, 'Whoever can live alone is either an animal or a god.'
>
> Well, I of course, am neither an animal nor a god and I remember the pride when I was a child of the Second World War of the Battle of Britain. The last few days here in Poland have just kind of shattered something within me in that this sense of collective unity, this sense of collective pride, this sense of having a tribe, this sense of having a culture you can be proud of - has arisen within me, and I've never been to Poland before, I can't tell you how strange a feeling it is that I have a sense of unity with people in a country I've never been in before. It tells me just how much has been taken away from us by these goddamn cultural Marxists, by the people who oppose the West, by the people who oppose any kind of pride in Western history. This sense of unity, this sense of purpose, this quiet resolution and willingness to defend what your ancestors fought to give you - I have not experienced it in many decades. And I have never, ever experienced it as an adult.
>
> Go out into the public square and say you're proud of the West, you're proud of the freedoms that were fought for, and you're proud of the sacrifices of your ancestors and you're

immediately a fascist and a Nazi. But here, this quiet unity, this quiet pride, this calm resolution, this celebration without giddiness - I have never seen it before. I feel almost, I hate to say born again, but almost as if something has broken within me that I have put up to defend myself against criticisms of unity, against criticisms of pride. It is an appalling thing to take away people's history. It is an appalling thing to take away people's pride. And it is appalling thing to take away their unity because I've never felt it more strongly than I've felt it today. Today we stand, divided we fall.[146]

Poland has withstood partition by Prussia, Russia, and Austria, 123 years of foreign occupation, invasion by Nazis and then Soviets, and the ravages of Communism. The national unity of the Poles is unmatched in all of the Western world, except for perhaps Hungary. Walls work, by the way, with 99.6% of illegal border crossings down in Hungary after the erection of a 325 mile, 13-foot-tall high fence equipped with razor wire[147]. Walls work even better.

American national identity will never look like it did before. The demographics guarantee it. But a total immigration moratorium for the better part of a generation would allow some measure of assimilation, relief for labor, and give the culture a chance to step out of the Third World deluge it has found itself in. The children will see less conflict in their schools. Traditions will come back to the fore and chip away at the strength of the welfare state. Religion may even see a resurgence, particularly of the Christian flavor. The country won't be awash in criminal illegal aliens and will find its attention has turned to pedophiles deeply embedded in the institutions. The pedophiles and child traffickers running America's major institutions want as open

---

[146] https://www.youtube.com/watch?v=V-YBpTCXTQ8
[147] https://en.s4c.news/2018/11/02/__trashed-3

borders as possible. To paraphrase Ann Coulter, no time to concentrate on mastermind level criminals when the society is awash with illegal alien Aztecs drunk on Tecate mowing down Kate Steinles. America may even recover some of its folkloric dimension, paying homage to the Founders, Lewis and Clark, and its patriotic inventors and tinkering businessmen of every stripe.

This unity is the state of normal affairs that marks nations like Poland and Hungary. Watch some YouTube videos on these places! There is social balance. Conservative figures can speak in public forums without fear for their personal safety. The banking and finance sectors aren't wholly run by parasitic international interests. The architecture communicates something about the people living there, not the whims of bureaucrats a thousand miles away. The food is locally sourced because big business hasn't been given endless subsidies to muscle out the little guy with. The natural spaces and wilderness areas are cherished because the people imagine their children and grandchildren inheriting the land. The music is natural, organic, and soothing because people are focused on having families, not doing drugs and having sloppy, protected sex. The national identity reveres great moral heroes who advanced the cause of the nation. The national identity of do it yourself, settler and pioneer mindset gives every man the meaning and purpose he needs to be effective in his own life, regardless of his intelligence or personal connections. The institutions are open and siphon up talent and hard work in order to deliver men back unto themselves, rather than devour them for selfish ends. The social environment redirects people back into the family.

American national identity could live again but first some moral courage is in order.

So long as a healthy measure of American national identity lives on the people, there is a chance for the West to reform itself after a Balkanization or in the face of a sustained diaspora status. The Poles endured what they had to. Americans and Americana will have to, as well.

Mobility Matters

The Jewish people have had to move from country to country, a selective pressure that has favored those with the most awareness of impending danger and an ability to transport their wealth with them. One example of this kind of resourcefulness comes from Felix Rohatyn, considered the "preeminent investment banker of his generation":

> I was twelve, the year was 1940, and my family - mother, grandmother, and our longtime Polish cook - were making our anxious and harried way south through Nazi-occupied France. With mattresses tied to the roof of our car, we had driven out of Paris with the makeshift plan of somehow getting across the Spanish border. Our entire 'fortune' consisted of a handful of gas coupons and a few Kolynos toothpaste tubes that, as my mother had instructed, I had emptied and then carefully refilled with dozens of gold coins.
>
> The road out of Paris was a nightmare. Stretching into the distance was a teeming stream of refugees, a confusion packed with automobiles, horse carts, bicycles, and those with no choice but to flee on foot. A day's progress was measured in just a few frustrating miles. Worse, there was always the fear of encountering a German checkpoint. We were Jews; and the rumors about what was happening in the Dachau "internment

camp" outside Munich had left us terrorized. I had no doubts about what the Nazis had in store for my family. Returning to German-occupied Paris, we feared, would be accepting a death sentence.[148]

Mr. Rohatyn and his family were able to achieve passage to America where Rohatyn remade the merger-and-acquisition business into what it is, attaining a dazzling fortune in the process. Rohatyn's mother saw the writing on the wall for Jews in occupied France and moved accordingly. Now her son languishes in splendid isolation on his sprawling ranch in Cora, Wyoming, staffed by outfitters, cooks, maids, and horse handlers - coming out to Jackson or Denver on occasion to be interviewed by Bloomberg or Fox News.

White Americans will not have a free market America to escape to. One can easily imagine some heinous, anti-white law passing in Baltimore, Detroit, Los Angeles, or New York City - forcing a mass exodus. This is already happening, on a quieter scale, with Oregon, California, New Mexico, Colorado, Illinois, Vermont, and Massachusetts serving as sanctuary states where illegal aliens, whose murder rate is seven times the native population (not adjusted for race), are legally shielded from deportation. Whites are fleeing the more urban of these states, heading toward the interior of the country where the legal systems retain some semblance of rationality.

---

[148] Rohatyn, F. G. (2013). Dealings: A political and financial life. Place of publication not identified: Simon & Schuster.

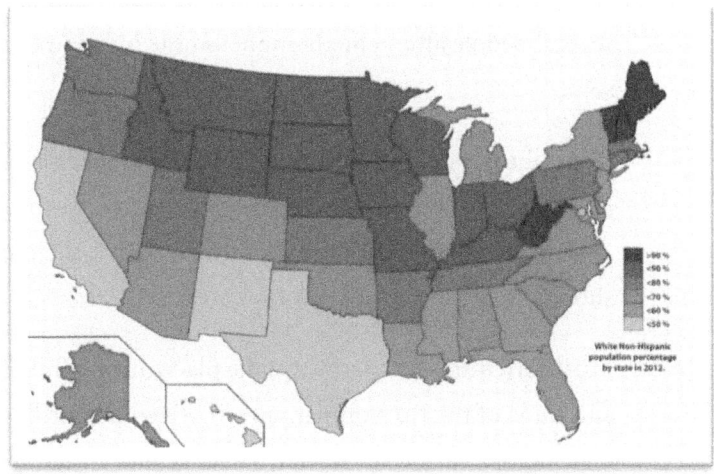

Maps of the States by non-Hispanic whites reveal a telling picture[149]. Whites are receding. There may be freedom of movement between the States at this point, but asset forfeiture and gun-seizure laws are on the rise. Asset forfeiture happens when state highway patrol pulls over a vehicle, for any reason under the legal sun, and discovers any amount of cash. The officer and his buddies then seize the cash, usually keeping it for their department's operating fund. South Dakota, in the heart of the White America of tomorrow, seized $1.3 million and 70 vehicles in 2018[150]. Typically, "the government has to be able to prove in a civil, administrative or criminal proceeding that the asset was used to facilitate drug trafficking or was derived from drug trafficking for it to be forfeited to the government[151]" but this isn't always what happens in practice. Utah is notorious for fickle asset seizure conduct:

> In one case highlighted by the Salt Lake Tribune, cops seized cars and other property—including "a $25 flashlight…a

---

[149] https://en.wikipedia.org/wiki/Non-Hispanic_whites
[150] https://atg.sd.gov/LawEnforcement/DrugAssetCivilForfeiture/default.aspx
[151] http://wyomingdci.wyo.gov/dci-operations-section/drug-seizures

$4,000 mountain bike, a $2,500 motorcycle and a guitar autographed by Led Zeppelin worth $3,000"— and charged several people after a methamphetamine bust, prosecutors say.

Cops like to publicize such busts because it feeds a narrative that asset forfeiture is used primarily against big-time drug dealers. But they're rather out of the ordinary, the report shows.

Most forfeitures (69 percent) take place during traffic stops and most of the time only money is seized. According to the state report, cash was taken in 99 percent of forfeitures during 2016, with the median seizure amounting to only $1,031.

That means, in many cases, the amount seized was considerably less than four-figures. In one instance, the report shows, police took $16 from a motorist.

"What are they doing where they have to take that $16 to protect public safety," says Jennifer McDonald, a research analyst for the Institute for Justice, a libertarian law firm that has challenged asset forfeiture laws in several states and advocates for reforms to the practice.

As in other places—like in Chicago, where cops have seized as little as 34 cents from motorists and targeted poor neighborhoods with forfeiture actions—the amount of the average seizure raises questions about how forfeiture is being used.

Small scale seizures give the victim almost no recourse. Under asset forfeiture laws, the burden of proof is on the property owner, and few people are going to hire a lawyer and go to court to recover a small amount of cash, McDonald says. "It's just ridiculous."

Important details about what has been taken—like the motorbike and the Led Zeppelin guitar—are only available from more detailed audits of asset forfeitures. Those audits are required in Arizona and Colorado, which recently passed forfeiture reforms that are the gold standard for states, McDonald says, but that's not required in Utah or many other places, for now.[152]

Victims of asset seizure, generally on interstate highways, are forced to hire lawyers in states where they don't reside to reclaim stolen goods totaling only $1,031 on average. One can imagine the type of feasting highway patrol departments across the American West and Midwest will partake in should there be a mass white exodus when the coastal states fall to Third World socialism and enact property seizure laws like the ones in South Africa.

Utah leads the way in asset seizure, if only because it is one of the few states required to make an annual report of asset seizure:

> Utah police seized about $2.2 million in cash last year under a law allowing authorities to take someone's property even if they aren't charged or convicted of a crime, a state report showed. The 2017 report on state asset forfeiture showed virtually all of the money and other assets seized by police

---

[152] https://reason.com/blog/2017/07/15/report-average-asset-forfeiture-just-103

came in drug investigations. In 13 percent of the cases, no criminal charges were filed.[153]

With IQ dropping across the country, the 13 percent figure will certainly climb as the years go by and Utah's police force becomes more and more Mexican.

Gun-seizure laws in the wake of mass shootings are on the rise:

> Following the Parkland school shooting, state lawmakers across the nation developed a newfound interest in a previously little-known means for separating volatile people from deadly weapons. Red flag laws — also known as Extreme Risk Protection Orders (ERPOs) or Gun Violence Restraining Orders (GVROs) — enable law enforcement, and sometimes family members and other concerned parties, to petition a judge to remove guns from individuals who pose a threat to themselves or others.[154]

Of course, these laws will be abused by liberals who know and dislike conservatives in their community. With the APA passing guidelines for mental health on toxic masculinity, which forbid straight men from taking risks or behaving with any sort of aggression (which is all too often simply assertiveness that liberals don't like), it is easy to see where gun seizure laws will go. Liberals are gun-grabbers and now they have the legal edicts of "mental health" on their side. No surprise to anyone, the states that have passed these so-called red flag laws are many of the same states that have rotten asset forfeiture laws or act as

---

[153] https://www.deseretnews.com/article/900024126/utah-police-seized-dollar22m-in-cash-under-civil-forfeiture-law.html

[154] https://www.thetrace.org/2018/03/red-flag-laws-pending-bills-tracker-nra/

sanctuary states: Oregon, California, Illinois, Vermont, Massachusetts, Rhode Island, and Utah.

The bunker down and fight to the death model of self-defense did not work for the Jews until they had their own homeland replete with nuclear capabilities, massive subsidies from America's military industrial complex, all manner of US foreign aid, and the sanction of the world's major empires. Only then did events such as the 1967 Arab-Israeli War become cakewalks for Israel. Should whites seek to establish their own homeland, the odds will not tilt so kindly in their favor lest a full-on systematic, *violent* white genocide happen somewhere. Whites who remain in liberal jurisdictions once America has passed its demographic cliff can expect to have their possessions and cash stripped, their guns taken through mental-health-buttressed gun seizure laws, and their avenues for white flight cut off by intermediary states like Illinois, Colorado, and New York (the first two blocking off the American West and the third blocking off the Northeast). Clandestine transfer of wealth out of hostile jurisdictions, not so different from Felix Rohatyn's placing gold coins in toothpaste tubes, will become the norm.

The Average Joe in America historically hasn't had to face the government predation that is rising up as the demographics shift to Third Worldism. This is changing. Media darling Alexandra Ocasio-Cortez wants a Green New Deal that will cost taxpayers over $100 trillion. Bernie Sanders waits in the wings as the Democratic frontrunner. Outsider Andrew Yang wants universal basic income. Every Democrat under the sun agrees on two things: whites should be taxed more, and the funds should be redistributed to minorities. Whites will need to figure out what mobility and wealth transfer means with these impending circumstances. The Jews were smart enough to do it in the 1940's. How far off is a 1940's scenario for whites? Not that far off. More on this in a moment.

Verbal, Not Physical

According to Jackie Mason:

In this country, Jews don't fight. I don't know if you noticed that. In this country they ALMOST fight. Every Jew I know ALMOST killed somebody. They'll all tell you. 'If he had said one more word...he would've been dead today. That's right. I was ready. One more word...' What's the word? Nobody knows what that word is.[155]

Jews are not known for their fighting prowess, despite their tremendous victories in the Arab-Israeli conflicts and the Warsaw Uprising, which lasted for 63 days with little outside support. Rabbi Telushkin writes:

> The early Zionist leader Shmaryahu Levin crystallized this timid self-perception in a revealing autobiographical reminiscence. One night, during the 1936 Arab riots in Palestine, Levin was walking alone down a street in Jerusalem when he saw an Arab coming toward him. Levin lifted the flap of his overcoat and covered his face.
>
> 'That way the Arab was frightened because he didn't know who was behind the coat -and I was frightened because I knew who was behind it.'

---

[155] Telushkin, J. (1992). Jewish humor: What the best Jewish jokes say about the Jews. New York: W. Morrow.

Whites have tremendous fighting prowess. They were all too eager to prove themselves in the World Wars, leading to the decimation of the most courageous fighting stock left in the Europeans. It comes as little surprise that martial prowess would recede from the forefront of the West as a survival strategy. The governments have untold weaponry they would happily unleash on bands of rebels. The American government has had decades of practice on Muslim terrorist cells they allowed into the country and would happily turn these tactics on to whichever group of concerned citizens had the gumption to plan military maneuvers. The recent Bundy family occupation of a BLM facility in rural Oregon only lasted because it was an isolated event covered non-stop by the media and because the taste of Waco and Ruby Ridge is still in the mouth of the average conservative. Decentralized uprisings occurring past some social tipping point will be all too easy to isolate and neutralize with military force, well out of sight of the cameras. The media needed the Bundy rebellion in order to paint Trump supporters as lunatics. The media won't need to prove anything to anyone once Third World socialism has fully taken over.

Stefan Molyneux writes, "High IQ whites have greater empathy (compared to the global average). It's why they created universal morality and ended the slave trade. It was a strength in the past, but now a weakness being horribly exploited.[156]" Higher IQ whites have also had world shaking martial power. It was a strength in the past, but the civilization wreckers have been clever in twisting it into a weakness that can be exploited. This is not to say that violence in self-defense must be forgone. It means that the social media algorithms and gatekeepers specifically target confrontational and antagonistic conservatives. There is an information war on a specific kind of conservative, the kind that is able to inspire a fighting spirit in

---

[156] https://twitter.com/StefanMolyneux/status/1103316815839543298

the audience. Social media and institutional deplatforming results in a dumbed down field of Conservative, Inc. and MAGA, Inc. grifters keeping the attention of mainstream conservatives while the "disruptors", as Michelle Malkin terms them, are kept in the dark. The prominent globalists leading major American industries did not come to prominence by stoking antagonism and confrontation in their audiences. They did so by keeping their cool and slowly changing society's narratives to their favor. The portion of them that have been "disruptors" at heart have been careful not to draw a certain kind of attention to themselves. Any James O'Keefe exposé will tell of their clandestine nature. Meanwhile, passionate whites are hurling themselves at the maw of the Silicon Valley beast in the hopes of rousing enough outrage in the voting populace so that better voting decisions will be made. This is effective but its effectiveness is blotted out by the superior effectiveness of public deplatforming.

Conservative political dissidents do well to take a page out of the books of the most intellectually powerful: those who run Conservative, Inc., entertainment, finance, the DNC, and so forth behind the scenes. These people long ago decided to no longer make martyrs of themselves, Jewish or not. The way forward is through reasoned, deliberate argumentation exposing the evils of the elite and the political activities required for peaceable victory. Whites will know when the switch has flipped, and this is no longer the way forward. Many are too eager to jump the gun, which only reveals important strategy to the enemy to the degree the person has climbed the white, conservative hierarchy. Let's hope open, sustained political violence never breaks out.

The strengths of whites have been manipulated into weaknesses. Whites will need to develop the low time preference that builds and builds the political will that ensures total victory. Nor is this some nefarious scheme. Whites are well known for wanting lassez-faire societies with equality under the law and freedoms of speech and association. There is no boogeyman lurking among conservatives. The lessons of WWII have been learned. Freedom and unbridled prosperity await but only if the political stratagem is carried out properly.

A cogent example for the need for temperance and sober low time preference comes from British Columbia:

> A Canadian jury has found a man guilty of manslaughter for killing another man with a single punch in a Starbucks.
>
> Lawrence Alvin Sharpe, 41, was convicted on Saturday in connection with the July 2017 death of Michael Page-Vincelli, 22, in Burnaby, British Columbia, a suburb of Vancouver.
>
> The same jury acquitted Sharpe's girlfriend, 36-year-old Oldouz Pournouruz, of provoking the attack, after the court heard that she had goaded Sharpe to beat up Page-Vincelli after her own dispute with the man.
>
> The incident unfolded in the parking lot of a shopping center, where Pournouruz and Page-Vincelli got into a verbal dispute while her boyfriend ran inside a bank. Witnesses said they saw Page-Vincelli and Pournouruz shouting at each other, reportedly after he took issue with her after she tossed a cigarette butt on the ground.
>
> Pournouruz claimed that Page-Vincelli called her a 'dirty immigrant' and told her to return to her home country before flicking his own lit cigarette at her.

The court heard that Page-Vincelli walked away from the argument and went into a nearby Starbucks, while Pournouruz ran inside the bank to tell Sharp of the dispute.

Surveillance video evidence from inside the coffee shop shows the couple walking into the Starbucks, where Pournouruz appears to point at Page-Vincelli.

Sharpe is seen sucker punching the 22-year-old, who falls backwards. As he fell, Page-Vincelli struck his head on the ground or possibly a counter, fracturing his skull.

He was rushed to a hospital, but later died of his injuries.[157]

Lawrence Alvin Sharpe and Oldouz Pournouruz may be Canadian citizens but they are not Westerners by any stretch of the imagination. Michael Page-Vincelli, however, was very much a Westerner and likely had a considerably higher IQ than his killer. In the Third World, one small comment makes the difference between life and death. Burnaby, Canada is becoming the Third World. Michael Page-Vincelli did not play by the new power rules of the West. He operated with the bravado-toward-the-outgroup rules of the past, the ones that faded soon after WWII. He was killed for failing to observe the simian code of conduct on the street level. He fought with idiots and was dragged down to their level and defeated. Michael Page-Vincelli will have no children. He has become a statistic in the staggering trend of black on white violent crime. If only a fellow white had been able to reach him in time with a discussion of the need for low time preference, temperance, and a commitment to institutional change. Western media is littered with stories of young white men and women

---

[157] https://www.dailymail.co.uk/news/article-6773551/Canadian-man-guilty-manslaughter-one-punch-death-inside-Starbucks.html

who died because they did not grasp the stakes or were misled into their own destruction.

It may seem at odds for me to write at length about the direness of the situation and the ticking clock of demographic winter yet advocate for a political strategy of patience and endurance, but this was the way the current elite assumed power, their reproduction rates falling like everyone else's. The difference here being that whites have precisely 25 years to do what others did in 70. We all know what is coming.

The Holocaust

The Holocaust looms large to the Jewish people as their "never again" moment. Never again will the Jewish people be exposed to wholesale slaughter at the hands of anyone. Strong-willed leaders have emerged for the Jewish people, armed with the knowledge of persecution and the need for absolute assurances of the continued survival of the Jewish people.

David Ben-Gurion oversaw the 1948 Arab-Israeli war, united the various Jewish militias into the Israel Defense Forces, and secured reparation payments from Germany for Nazi Germany's confiscation of Jewish property during WWII. Golda Meir, known as a chain-smoking lioness, steered Israel through the Yom Kippur War in 1973, directed IDF commandos to exact reprisals on Palestinians responsible for the 1972 Munich Olympics massacre of Israeli athletes, and was famously called "the best man in the government" by David Ben-Gurion. Benjamin Netanyahu famously served in the Israel Defense Forces as the leader of a special forces unit, serving during several crucial operations, before becoming Israel's youngest Prime Minister ever - now having served as Prime Minister four times.

The Holocaust has survived as a motivating catalyst for Jewish leaders and others to create a homeland in Israel protected by the Samson Option, "an all-out (nuclear) attack against an adversary should defenses fail and population centers be threatened.[158]" Mutually assured destruction is what prevented the Cold War from turning hot and it will be the doctrine that ensures Israel will never be conquered from without. The Jewish people will never again succumb to a genocidal outside force.

Whites, nor any nationality of whites, have this degree of cohesion and sense of self-preservation - aside from the Poles, Hungarians, and perhaps the Italians. None of these nations possess nuclear weapons, though Italy hosted them in the past as part of NATO and Poland has discussed gaining access to nuclear technology as part of a self-preservation strategy[159]. Whites have not had their "never again" moment. Since most people learn not from prosperity but from hardship, it is increasingly difficult to envision a path to self-assurance for whites that does not involve some measure of mass die-off. The domestication of consumer credit runs deep. Jewish consumer credit in the 1940's ran dry and alternative measures were vigorously pursued to overwhelming success. Jewish self-preservation runs so deep it has even peaked through into popular culture, making an appearance in the popular film World War Z where Israel has managed to survive a zombie apocalypse (metaphor for mass migration) through towering walls and a thorough checkpoint system manned by trained soldiers. With 76,000 illegal aliens crossing

---

[158] https://www.globalsecurity.org/wmd/world/israel/doctrine.htm
[159] https://www.theguardian.com/world/2015/dec/06/poland-considering-asking-for-access-to-nuclear-weapons-under-nato-program

America's southern border last month, the highest number in 12 years[160], it remains to be seen if American whites will stave off a "never again" moment or bring one upon themselves through apathy and a deferral to corrupt politicians in Congress.

That Which Contributes To The Community

Amy Chua's book *Political Tribes* is quick to point out that America's elite have lost sight of the group identities that matter deeply to Americans much like they were blind to the power of tribal politics overseas during the Obama, Bush, and Clinton era of foreign interventionism and regime change. America's WASPS, in an effort to allay the malefices of identity politics succeeded only in removing themselves from the halls of power. The Jewish people have not been so foolish. Rabbi Telushkin writes:

> The real question that jokes about (Jewish) materialism raises is this: How is wealth regarded within the Jewish community? The answer: with great respect, provided it leads to communal and charitable involvement. Indeed, wealth plays a major, often THE major, role in the assignment of community honors. Jewish organizations hold annual banquets to honor wealthy donors, even when other people have worked harder and contributed a higher percentage of their income."

---

[160] https://nypost.com/2019/03/05/yeah-this-looks-like-a-border-crisis/?utm_source=twitter_sitebuttons&utm_medium=site%20buttons&utm_campaign=site%20buttons

Americans are by far and away the most charitable people in the world, giving a record $410 billion to charity in 2017 on the strength of the Trump economy[161]. One look at a charitable giving map reveals a correlation between religiosity and charity, with the coastal liberal states lagging far behind flyover states on percentage of adjusted gross income given to charity[162]. Utah leads the nation at 6.61% on the strength of the Latter-Day Saint policy of tithing, a commandment that adherents give 10% of their income to the church for charitable works. The nation's foremost example of charitable giving involves some measure of Mormon in-group preference. The religion's adherents are largely white, for the short time being, as the church is dedicated to international outreach at an unprecedented scale[163] - focusing the majority of its efforts on Central and South America and Brazil. There is no explicit in-group preference for ethnic Europeans among Forbes' top ten charities for 2018[164]:

1. United Way

2. Feed America

3. Americares Foundation

4. Task Force For Global Health

---

[161] https://givingusa.org/giving-usa-2018-americans-gave-410-02-billion-to-charity-in-2017-crossing-the-400-billion-mark-for-the-first-time/

[162] "U.S. charitable giving map: How and where Americans donate" https://www.rawhide.org/blog/infographics/charitable-giving-map/?gclid=Cj0KCQiAn4PkBRCDARIsAGHmH3cjGBIsMvkX3x_FhpAelhTPJ5G1DdWmRJLu8vAaC3dlmuwYFtD9iCMaAonoEALw_wcB

[163] "What huge numbers for LDS video say about international outreach" https://www.deseretnews.com/article/865626080/What-huge-numbers-for-LDS-video-say-about-churchs-international-outreach.html

[164] https://www.forbes.com/lists/top-charities/#4a9893035f50

5. The Salvation Army

6. St. Jude Children's Research Hospital

7. Direct Relief

8. Habitat For Humanity

9. Boys & Girls Clubs of America

10. YMCA of the USA

Some of these charities explicitly base the scope of their work in America, which still has a non-Hispanic white majority at 60.7%[165] and dropping rapidly, and therefore benefit whites by proxy. A look at some of the most successful Jewish charities operating in America paints a different picture. The Jewish Federations of North America states in its mission, "The Jewish Federations of North America raise and distribute more than $3 billion annually for social welfare, social services and educational needs. The Federation movement protects and enhances the well-being of Jews worldwide.[166]" The United Jewish Appeal-Federation of Jewish Philanthropies of New York, which raised $299.4 million in 2018[167], dedicates 42% of its funds to three categories that are explicitly Jewish: Strengthening Jewish Life, Investing In Israeli Society, and Creating Inclusive Jewish Communities. The Birthright Israel Foundation seeks to ensure:

> -that every eligible young Jewish adult around the world, especially the less connected, is given the opportunity to visit Israel on this educational journey. Birthright Israel Foundation raises funds in the United States to support

---

[165] https://www.census.gov/quickfacts/fact/table/US/PST045217
[166] https://jewishfederations.org/how-federations-help
[167] https://eaf.ujafedny.org/assets/UJA_AR_2018_HQ.pdf

Birthright Israel. The Birthright Israel program aims to give the gift of an educational trip to Israel to 50,000 young Jewish adults each year.[168]

The charitable organization is highly active, listing assets of $96,908,000 and total expenses of $93,803,000 for the year 2017.

There are no major charitable organizations in America dedicated to the "well-being of whites worldwide", to "Investing In A White Society", or sending whites to their ethnic homelands back in Europe as means of encouraging high marriage rates and fealty to Western ideals. This very notion is enough to arouse racial resentment against whites from every corner of the globe yet the Jewish people, who are often confused for whites (and who often deliberately confuse others by pretending to be whites), persist quietly in their efforts to enrich their own community - whether out of racial sentiments or more identitarian considerations of tribe. Whites stand to learn much from the concentrated charitable giving of the Jewish community: the Jews give to their own. This should be emulated, not vilified. Obviously, Jewish organizations give humanitarian aid to all peoples, but they do not give up their Jewish core because of leftist political pressures. The United Jewish Appeal has hosted speakers such as Ronald Reagan and Theresa May at luncheons. It is not a bigoted organization just the same as an explicitly white charity involved in parallel work for whites would not be. The world may not be ready to accept this reality and may, in fact, rouse every means at its disposal to prevent white ethnocentric charity but the principle remains: if Jews can do it, so can whites.

A diaspora mindset will be precisely what prevents whites from becoming a diaspora.

---

[168] https://birthrightisrael.foundation/mission

Let's do something now so we won't have to see what will happen to us in the forced labor camps to come.

Made in the USA
Las Vegas, NV
14 December 2020